THE COVENANT

Retreat Leader Guide
WORKBOOK

RICHARD T. CASE

Acknowledgments

I wish to dedicate this course to and thank all of the leaders of our **Ministry: Living Waters—ABIDE Ministries!** for walking together with my wife, Linda and I into this Covenant Life! These leaders faithfully have processed with us to receive that the life of God will all His children is the Covenant—blessed to be a blessing: always a flow through process whereby we receive all the promised blessings of the Covenant life and then are asked to give it away to others; and that those that join us (bless us) are blessed and those that do not join us (curse us and oppose us) are not, but we need not be burdened by that but leave that all up to God and thus can live in freedom always in all our relationships—a key part of the Covenant. Our leaders have fully embraced this and are being blessed as they give it away—and literally hundreds of others are now receiving it and giving it away. Why the Covenant is so important to the church—God's way of multiplication of His beautiful life—one life at a time. Thank you all:

These leaders are:

Jake & Mary Beckel:
Joe & Leigh Bogar
Rich & Janet Cocchiaro
Larry & Sherry Collet
David & Melissa Dunkel
Tom & Susanne Ewing
Rick & Kelly Ferris
Joel & Christina Gunn
Scott & Terry Hitchcock
Chris & Jaclyn Hoover
Rick & Nancy Hoover
Tad & Monica Jones
Ed & Becky Kobel
Don & Rachelle Light
Chris and Heidi May
Terry & Josephine Noetzel
Steve & Carolyn Van Ooteghem
Preston & Lynda Pitts
Dan & Kathy Rocconi
Bob & Keri Rockwell
John & Michelle Santaferraro
Allyson & Denny Weinberg
Neal & Kathy Weisenburger

Further, it is a joy for me to share this Covenant life with my wife, Linda, and family who together are enjoying the fruits of the Covenant. What an honor and a privilege for us.

THE COVENANT
PUBLISHED BY LIVING WATERS—ABIDE MINISTRIES
7615 Lemon Gulch Way
Castle Rock, CO 80108

Unless otherwise noted, all Scripture quotations are from the ESV® Bible (The Holy Bible, English Standard Version®), copyright © 2001 by Crossway Bibles, a publishing ministry of Good News Publishers. Used by permission. All rights reserved.

ISBN: 978-1-7360588-0-0
Copyright © 2024 by Richard T. Case.

All rights reserved. No part of this publication may be reproduced, distributed or transmitted in any form or by any means, including photocopying, recording, or other electronic or mechanical methods, without the prior written permission of the publisher.

Publisher's Cataloging-in-Publication data

Names:
Title:
Description: .
Identifiers: ISBN | LCCN
Subjects:

Printed in the United States of America 2024 — 2ND ed

TABLE OF CONTENTS

Introduction 1

Lesson One:
The Key Elements of the Covenant 4

Lesson Two:
The Privileges of the Covenant 22

Lesson Three:
The Privileges of the Covenant (*Con't.*) 36

Lesson Four:
Our Responsibilities in This Agreement 48

Lesson Five:
Our Responsibilities in This Agreement (*Con't.*) 64

Lesson Six:
Our Responsibilities in This Agreement (*Con't.*) 78

Lesson Seven:
Our Responsibilities in This Agreement (*Con't.*) 92

Lesson Eight:
Called to Give It Away (Be a Blessing) 108

THE COVENANT

INTRODUCTION

"I will bless you so you will be a blessing"

—Genesis 12:2

INTRODUCTION

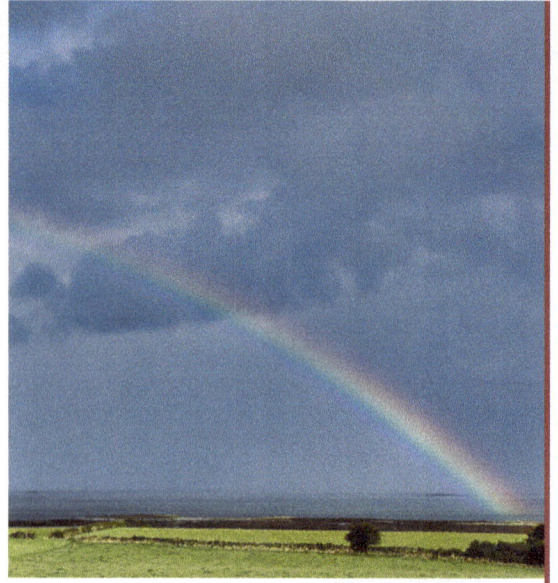

Write out what you think is the primary purpose of God's eternal covenant for you? Where do you believe you are experiencing this? What questions do you have regarding the application of the covenant for your life right now? Where do you believe you are struggling keeping up your side of the covenant?

_____
_____
_____
_____
_____
_____
_____
_____
_____
_____
_____
_____
_____
_____
_____
_____
_____
_____
_____
_____
_____
_____
_____
_____

INTRODUCTION

LESSON 1:
THE KEY ELEMENTS OF THE COVENANT

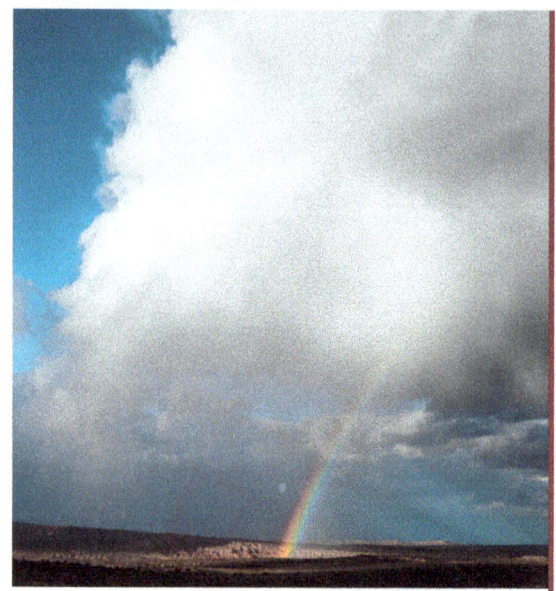

1. WHAT IS THE ESSENCE OF THE COVENANT (THE FATHER'S AGREEMENT)?

> **Read through Genesis 12:1-3 and write out the essence and elements of the covenant:**
>
> The Call of Abram
> **12** Now the Lord said[a] to Abram, "Go from your country[b] and your kindred and your father's house to the land that I will show you. **2** And I will make of you a great nation, and I will bless you and make your name great, so that you will be a blessing. **3** I will bless those who bless you, and him who dishonors you I will curse, and in you all the families of the earth shall be blessed."[c]

> "Throughout this study we will come to understand that we are to be blessed to give that blessing away and be a blessing to others"

_____
_____
_____
_____
_____
_____
_____
_____

The covenant is an agreement between the Father and His children, and it is very simple: He will bless us to make us a blessing; and He will bless those who bless us and curse those who curse us. Throughout this study we will come to understand that we are to be blessed to give that blessing away and be a blessing to others; and will further understand the importance of blessing those who bless us and cursing those who curse us. The covenant is all this. Keep this in mind throughout the course as we go into the depth of all that this means.

LESSON 1:
THE KEY ELEMENTS OF THE COVENANT

Word Meanings: **Blessing:** prosperity
Make: to act, act with effect, effect;

2. WHY IS THIS COVENANT THE BASIS OF THE FATHER'S RELATIONSHIP WITH HIS CHILDREN HERE ON EARTH?

There are eternal reasons why the covenant is the basis of the Father's fundamental relationship with His children here on Earth. It is our role to understand the overarching reason why the covenant defines this relationship:

REASON ONE: To glorify Himself.

> **Read through 1 Chronicles 16:8-30 and write out all the purposes or aspects of why God gives His people the covenant. How do we fulfill this as we experience the covenant?**
>
> David's Song of Thanks
> 8 Oh give thanks to the Lord; call upon his name;
>   make known his deeds among the peoples!
> 9 Sing to him, sing praises to him;
>   tell of all his wondrous works!
> 10 Glory in his holy name;
>   let the hearts of those who seek the Lord rejoice!
> 11 Seek the Lord and his strength;
>   seek his presence continually!
> 12 Remember the wondrous works that he has done,
>   his miracles and the judgments he uttered,
> 13 O offspring of Israel his servant,
>   children of Jacob, his chosen ones!
> 14 He is the Lord our God;
>   his judgments are in all the earth.
> 15 Remember his covenant forever,
>   the word that he commanded, for a thousand generations,
> 16 the covenant that he made with Abraham,
>   his sworn promise to Isaac,
> 17 which he confirmed to Jacob as a statute,
>   to Israel as an everlasting covenant,

LESSON 1:
THE KEY ELEMENTS OF THE COVENANT

> [18] saying, "To you I will give the land of Canaan,
>   as your portion for an inheritance."
> [19] When you were few in number,
> of little account, and sojourners in it,
> [20] wandering from nation to nation,
>   from one kingdom to another people,
> [21] he allowed no one to oppress them;
>   he rebuked kings on their account,
> [22] saying, "Touch not my anointed ones,
>   do my prophets no harm!"
> [23] Sing to the Lord, all the earth!
>   Tell of his salvation from day to day.
> [24] Declare his glory among the nations,
>   his marvelous works among all the peoples!
> [25] For great is the Lord, and greatly to be praised,
>   and he is to be feared above all gods.
> [26] For all the gods of the peoples are worthless idols,
>   but the Lord made the heavens.
> [27] Splendor and majesty are before him;
>   strength and joy are in his place.
> [28] Ascribe to the Lord, O families of the peoples,
>   ascribe to the Lord glory and strength!
> [29] Ascribe to the Lord the glory due his name;
>   bring an offering and come before him!
> Worship the Lord in the splendor of holiness;[a]
> [30] tremble before him, all the earth;
>   yes, the world is established; it shall never be moved.

_____
_____
_____
_____
_____
_____

LESSON 1:
THE KEY ELEMENTS OF THE COVENANT

The covenant brings glory to God. The wonderful, miraculous, supernatural works of God through His blessing us in the covenant are intended to bring glory to Him and thus to bring our praises to Him. Spend some time on verse 27 and work through the four qualities of being in God's presence: honor, majesty, strength (supernatural miracles), and gladness (joy). If we are experiencing the covenant, we will be experiencing these qualities and by definition giving God the glory. The covenant is never about us but always about Him.

Word Meanings:

Wondrous Works: be marvelous, be wonderful, be surpassing, be extraordinary, separate by distinguishing action
Glory: to shine (*figuratively of God's favor*), to flash forth light, to praise, boast, be boastful
Praised: same as glory
Gladness: joy
Strength: might
Honor: splendor, majesty

REASON TWO: To elevate our life to the spiritual: live in heaven while on Earth, which is under the control of the enemy, bear witness to the truth and covenant

---

Read through Ephesians 1:3-6, 1:13-14 and write out what happens to our life as we experience the covenant. How does this happen, and to what will we bear witness to and why?

Spiritual Blessings in Christ
³ Blessed be the God and Father of our Lord Jesus Christ, who has blessed us in Christ with every spiritual blessing in the heavenly places, ⁴ even as he chose us in him before the foundation of the world, that we should be holy and blameless before him. In love ⁵ he predestined us[a] for adoption to himself as sons through Jesus Christ, according to the purpose of his will, ⁶ to the praise of his glorious grace, with which he has blessed us in the Beloved.

¹³ In him you also, when you heard the word of truth, the gospel of your salvation, and believed in him, were sealed with the promised Holy Spirit, ¹⁴ who is the guarantee[a] of our inheritance until we acquire possession of it,[b] to the praise of his glory.

LESSON 1:
THE KEY ELEMENTS OF THE COVENANT

_____
_____
_____
_____
_____

We are to be lifted up to live life in the spiritual realms (heaven) and not be limited to just the natural life on Earth. We have been blessed with every spiritual blessing from heaven and are to live this out according to His purpose, which is to be living in the covenant. By definition this only happens as we are living in the spiritual dimension where the covenant can be fulfilled. This means that if we only live in the natural, in the flesh, it will not be fulfilled, which is why God intended to use the covenant to elevate our lives to the spiritual. Further, we are sealed with the Holy Spirit as a guarantee that we can live out this life in the spiritual. Thus, it is our privilege to be living in His power and be the recipient of the covenant because of this privilege, and always be lifted up to live life in the spiritual.

Word Meanings:

Blessing: to cause to prosper, to make happy, to bestow blessings on, favored of God, blessed

Spiritual: belonging to the Divine Spirit, of God the Holy Spirit, one who is filled with and governed by the Spirit of God

Blessings: speaking, fine speeches (what God speaks from heaven that creates physical things)

Heaven: heavenly origin or nature

Pleasure: good will, kindly intent, benevolence, delight, satisfaction

Will: what one wishes or has determined shall be done, of the purpose of God to bless mankind through Christ, of what God wishes to be done by us

Word: uttered by a living voice, embodies a conception or idea of what someone has said, a word, the sayings of God

Truth: what is true in any matter under consideration, truly, in truth, according to truth of a truth, in reality, in fact, certainly

Believed: to think to be true, to be persuaded of, to credit, place confidence in, of the thing believed, to credit, have confidence

Sealed: to set a seal upon, mark with a seal, to seal, for security: from Satan, since things sealed up are concealed (as the contents of a letter), to hide, keep in silence, keep secret, in order to mark a person or a thing, to set a mark upon by the impress of a seal or a stamp

LESSON 1:
THE KEY ELEMENTS OF THE COVENANT

Word Meanings: **Guarantee:** money that in purchases is given as a pledge or down payment that the full amount will subsequently be paid
Inheritance: property received (or to be received) by inheritance

Read through and write out what the church's (we believers) true purpose is in living out the covenant. To whom do we demonstrate this? Thus, what has to happen in order for this to be demonstrated, and what are we in turn experiencing?

> **Read Ephesians 3:8-13.**
>
> 8 To me, though I am the very least of all the saints, this grace was given, to preach to the Gentiles the unsearchable riches of Christ, 9 and to bring to light for everyone what is the plan of the mystery hidden for ages in[a] God, who created all things, 10 so that through the church the manifold wisdom of God might now be made known to the rulers and authorities in the heavenly places. 11 This was according to the eternal purpose that he has realized in Christ Jesus our Lord, 12 in whom we have boldness and access with confidence through our faith in him. 13 So I ask you not to lose heart over what I am suffering for you, which is your glory.

_____
_____
_____
_____
_____

As we are living life in the spiritual, we will be experiencing the supernatural because of the covenant, and thus will be demonstrating to the powers and principalities that the wonderful works of God are true and real. This is our calling, and why the covenant is such an important part of our relationship to God. If it is happening at that level, it obviously will impact other people who will have a desire to know more about the truth and knowing God as well. Our calling is not to tell other people "about God" but to live in the covenant where we will be manifesting the power of God to principalities and powers; and thus, to people who will want to know God.

LESSON 1:
THE KEY ELEMENTS OF THE COVENANT

Word Meanings:

Unsearchable Riches: that which cannot be searched out, that which cannot be comprehended—fullness, abundance, plenitude

Fellowship: the share which one has in anything, participation, intercourse, intimacy Known: shown in reality

Manifold: much, large, significant

Wisdom: which belongs to men, the varied knowledge of things human and divine, acquired by acuteness and experience, the act of interpreting dreams and always giving the sagest advice, the intelligence evinced in discovering the meaning of some mysterious number or vision, skill in the management of affairs, devout and proper prudence in intercourse with men not disciples of Christ, skill and discretion in imparting Christian truth, the knowledge and practice of the requisites for godly and upright living

---

Read Deuteronomy 28:13.

[13] And the Lord will make you the head and not the tail, and you shall only go up and not down, if you obey the commandments of the Lord your God, which I command you today, being careful to do them…

_____
_____
_____
_____

As we live in the covenant, we will be the head and not the tail and will be in a place of authority, experiencing His mighty power, and never to be subservient to anything else other than His authority and power. This means that we are never to accept mediocrity or to be subjugated to the enemy, to other people, or to other situations that would dominate us.

Word Meanings:

Head: top, summit, upper part, chief, total, sum, height, front, beginning

Tail: end, stump

Above: higher part, upper part (*substantive*), above (*adverb*), on the top of, on higher ground

Below: downwards, under

LESSON 1:
THE KEY ELEMENTS OF THE COVENANT

REASON THREE: To give it away.

> **Read through Genesis 12:3 and write out the bigger reason we are receiving of God's blessings. Why? What then does this mean is always part of the covenant?**
>
> ³ I will bless those who bless you, and him who dishonors you I will curse, and in you all the families of the earth shall be blessed."[a]

_____

_____

_____

_____

_____

    By definition the covenant is to make us a blessing and we are, in turn, to give that blessing away. It is a flow-through process. We never are just to receive the blessing but always to be in a position where as we receive the blessing we are to give it away, as so directed by Him.

Word Meanings: **Blessing:** prosperity
Make: to act, act with effect, effect

> **Read through and write out who actually becomes the covenant. What happens when others receive what we give away in our covenant life? By definition, what does that mean we are experiencing? Read Isaiah 42:6-7.**
>
> ⁶ "I am the Lord; I have called you[a] in righteousness;
>   I will take you by the hand and keep you;
> I will give you as a covenant for the people,
>   a light for the nations,
> ⁷ to open the eyes that are blind,
> to bring out the prisoners from the dungeon,
>   from the prison those who sit in darkness.

LESSON 1:
THE KEY ELEMENTS OF THE COVENANT

_____
_____
_____
_____
_____
_____

When we are part of God's covenant, we actually are to share ourselves with others, to open up blind eyes and bring light to help those who are bound up and in darkness to be led to freedom. When we are part of the covenant, we will be living in the covenant and then helping others to see the beauty of the covenant and have a heart to experience the covenant themselves. Then, they learn how to receive and live in the covenant; and then, like you, they will give it away to others. Thus, we become "the covenant."

Word Meanings: **Light:** of life, light of prosperity, light of instruction
Keep: to watch, guard, to preserve, guard from dangers, observe, guard with fidelity

> **Read through 1 Peter 2:9-10 and write out what these verses say about all of our roles as followers of Christ. What does this specifically mean? How do we carry out this role in everyday life?**
>
> [9] But you are a chosen race, a royal priesthood, a holy nation, a people for his own possession, that you may proclaim the excellencies of him who called you out of darkness into his marvelous light. [10] Once you were not a people, but now you are God's people; once you had not received mercy, but now you have received mercy.

_____
_____
_____
_____
_____

LESSON 1:
THE KEY ELEMENTS OF THE COVENANT

This reveals why we all are called as priest and are part of the royal priesthood. The primary role of the priest is to understand the will of God and then communicate that to others. Since we know that the primary will of God is for all of us to live in the covenant, our primary role as priest is to first live in the covenant and then communicate that to others, to give it away!

Chosen: ordained, appointed, choice, select, i.e. the best of its kind or class, royal, kingly, regal

Priest: the office of a priest (to understand the will of God and communicate that to the people and help them understand it; and teach the truth of God and help them understand it)

Proclaim: to tell out or forth, to declare abroad, divulge, publish, to make known by praising or proclaiming, to celebrate

Darkness: of ignorance respecting divine things and human duties, and the accompanying ungodliness and immorality, together with their consequent misery in hell, persons in whom darkness becomes visible and holds sway

Marvelous: extraordinary, striking, surprising, wonderful

Light: God is light because light has the extremely delicate, subtle, pure, brilliant quality of truth and its knowledge, together with the spiritual purity associated with it that which is exposed to the view of all, openly, publicly

3. WHO IS THE RECIPIENT OF THE COVENANT? HIS SPECIAL PEOPLE—HIS TREASURE.

Read through Deuteronomy 7:6-11 and write out to which people the verses are referring. What does this mean in relation to how the Father views us? Why is that important to us?

[6] "For you are a people holy to the Lord your God. The Lord your God has chosen you to be a people for his treasured possession, out of all the peoples who are on the face of the earth. [7] It was not because you were more in number than any other people that the Lord set his love on you and chose you, for you were the fewest of all peoples, [8] but it is because the Lord loves you and is keeping the oath that he swore to your fathers, that the Lord has brought you out with a mighty hand and redeemed you from the house of slavery, from the hand of Pharaoh king of Egypt. [9] Know therefore that the Lord your God is God, the faithful God who keeps covenant

LESSON 1:
THE KEY ELEMENTS OF THE COVENANT

> and steadfast love with those who love him and keep his commandments, to a thousand generations, ¹⁰ and repays to their face those who hate him, by destroying them. He will not be slack with one who hates him. He will repay him to his face. ¹¹ You shall therefore be careful to do the commandment and the statutes and the rules that I command you today.

_____
_____
_____
_____
_____

All of His children are recipients of the covenant but not just because we are His children, but because we are special to Him—His treasure. He values us and considers us His most precious gift, which is why He desires to bless us and have us bless others in the process.

Word Meanings:

Holy: sacred, Holy One, saint, set apart
Special People: possession, property, valued property, peculiar treasure
Covenant Loyalty: goodness, kindness, faithfulness

> **Read through Romans 8:12-17 and write out those privileges we are given as one of His children. How should we then be relating to God our Father and viewing His desire for us to live in the covenant?**
>
> Heirs with Christ
> ¹² So then, brothers,[a] we are debtors, not to the flesh, to live according to the flesh. ¹³ For if you live according to the flesh you will die, but if by the Spirit you put to death the deeds of the body, you will live. ¹⁴ For all who are led by the Spirit of God are sons[b] of God. ¹⁵ For you did not receive the spirit of slavery to fall back into fear, but you have received the Spirit of adoption as sons, by whom we cry, "Abba! Father!" ¹⁶ The Spirit himself bears witness with our spirit that we are children of God, ¹⁷ and if children, then heirs—heirs of God and fellow heirs with Christ, provided we suffer with him in order that we may also be glorified with him.

LESSON 1:
THE KEY ELEMENTS OF THE COVENANT

_____
_____
_____
_____
_____

As His children, He promises to lead and guide us; and to continually bear witness that we are His children, His special treasure. He wants us to fully receive our identity as children and recognize that it is our privilege to be His children. In turn, we always are to live in the covenant relationship He promises. We all are included; no one is exempt from receiving the full benefit of the covenant.

Word Meanings: **Children/Son of God:** used to describe Adam (Luke 3:38), used to describe those who are born again (Luke 20:36), and of angels, and of Jesus Christ, of those whom God esteems as sons, whom He loves, protects, and benefits above others, in the Old Testament used of the Jews, in the New Testament of Christians, those whose character God, as a loving Father, shapes by chastisements (Hebrews 12:5-8), those who revere God as their Father, the pious worshippers of God, those who in character and life resemble God, those who are governed by the Spirit of God, repose the same calm and joyful trust in God, which children do in their parents (Romans 8:14, Galatians 3:26), and hereafter in the blessedness and glory of the life eternal will openly wear this dignity of the sons of God. Term used preeminently of Jesus Christ, as enjoying the supreme love of God, united to Him in affectionate intimacy, privy to His saving councils, obedient to the Father's will in all His acts.

4. WHERE DOES THE COVENANT OPERATE? HIS SPECIAL PLACE—HIS KINGDOM.

> **Read through Luke 1:30-33 and write out your understanding of what Christ brought when He came to the world to demonstrate God's love and life for all of us, His creation. What does this mean, and why is this important to us as we now are walking with Him and living in this world?**
>
> [30] And the angel said to her, "Do not be afraid, Mary, for you have found favor with God. [31] And behold, you will conceive in your womb and bear a son, and you shall

LESSON 1:
THE KEY ELEMENTS OF THE COVENANT

> call his name Jesus. ³² He will be great and will be called the Son of the Most High. And the Lord God will give to him the throne of his father David, ³³ and he will reign over the house of Jacob forever, and of his kingdom there will be no end."

_____
_____
_____
_____
_____

Christ came to redeem us—to die on the cross and be resurrected so that we can again live with Him. Our problem with sin was resolved because of His love and grace toward us as He took care of the problem of sin Himself. He now offers this solution to those who believe what He did and—upon believing—are "born again." Then, we enter again into this restored eternal relationship. He brought His Kingdom to us so that as we now live in this relationship during our lifetime in this world, we can live out a covenant life with the benefits of the covenant. These are given in the Kingdom, where His power reigns and operates—His spiritual place of life where the covenant life is given to us.

Word Meanings:

Throne Seat: a chair of state having a footstool, assigned in the New Testament to kings, hence, kingly power or royalty, metaphor to God, the governor of the world, to the Messiah, Christ, the partner and assistant in the divine administration, hence divine power belonging to Christ, to judges (i.e., tribunal or bench,), to elders

Reign: to exercise the highest influence, to control

Kingdom: royal power, kingship, dominion, rule, not to be confused with an actual kingdom but rather the right or authority to rule over a kingdom. Of the royal power of Jesus as the triumphant Messiah, of the royal power and dignity conferred on Christians in the Messiah's Kingdom, the territory subject to the rule of a king, used in the New Testament to refer to the reign of the Messiah

LESSON 1:
THE KEY ELEMENTS OF THE COVENANT

> **Read through Luke 11:1-3 and write out what Christ tells us to ask for in our prayer life. Why is this so important to understand in relation to receiving His covenant life?**
>
> The Lord's Prayer
> **11** Now Jesus[a] was praying in a certain place, and when he finished, one of his disciples said to him, "Lord, teach us to pray, as John taught his disciples." **2** And he said to them, "When you pray, say:
> "Father, hallowed be your name.
> Your kingdom come.
> **3** Give us each day our daily bread…[b]

_____
_____
_____
_____
_____

It is not guaranteed we live in His Kingdom but have to ask for it—and for His will to be done there.

Word Meanings: **Kingdom:** royal power, kingship, dominion, rule, not to be confused with an actual kingdom but rather the right or authority to rule over a kingdom. Of the royal power of Jesus as the triumphant Messiah, of the royal power and dignity conferred on Christians in the Messiah's Kingdom, the territory subject to the rule of a king, used in the New Testament to refer to the reign of the Messiah

LESSON 1:
THE KEY ELEMENTS OF THE COVENANT

> **Read through Luke 8:9-10 and write out what we are privileged to receive in the Kingdom of God. Why is this so important as we are to receive God's covenant life?**
>
> The Purpose of the Parables
> ⁹ And when his disciples asked him what this parable meant, ¹⁰ he said, "To you it has been given to know the secrets of the kingdom of God, but for others they are in parables, so that 'seeing they may not see, and hearing they may not understand.'

_____
_____
_____
_____
_____

If the special privileges of being in the Kingdom and receiving the covenant is that we have access to mysteries and secret revelation that help us understand the deeper meanings of the covenant.

Word Meanings: **Mysteries:** hidden thing, secret, confided only to the initiated and not to ordinary mortals, not obvious to the understanding, hidden purpose, or counsel, secret will, the secret counsels which govern God in dealing with the righteous, which are hidden from ungodly and wicked men but plain to the godly in rabbinic writings, it denotes the mystic or hidden sense of an Old Testament saying of an image or form seen in a vision or a dream
Kingdom: royal power, kingship, dominion, rule, not to be confused with an actual kingdom but rather the right or authority to rule over a kingdom. of the royal power of Jesus as the triumphant Messiah, of the royal power and dignity conferred on Christians in the Messiah's Kingdom, the territory subject to the rule of a king, used in the New Testament to refer to the reign of the Messiah

LESSON 1:
THE KEY ELEMENTS OF THE COVENANT

> **Read through Psalm 93:1-2 and write out who reigns and has all the power in the Kingdom. Why is this so important to us to have settled and then be motivated to live in the Kingdom to let this power deliver to us the life of the covenant?**
>
> The Lord Reigns
> **93** The Lord reigns; he is robed in majesty;
>   the Lord is robed; he has put on strength as his belt.
> Yes, the world is established; it shall never be moved.
> **2** Your throne is established from of old;
>   you are from everlasting.

_____
_____
_____
_____
_____

God reigns (has the power and might to provide the benefits of the covenant), and we are to subject ourselves to His leadership and sovereignty in delivering His covenant to us. This only happens when He reigns in His Kingdom.

Word Meanings: **Reign:** counsel, advise, to consider
Throne: a chair of state having a footstool, assigned in the New Testament to kings, hence, kingly power or royalty, metaphor to God, the governor of the world, to the Messiah, Christ, the partner and assistant in the divine administration, hence divine power belonging to Christ, to judges (i.e., tribunal or bench), to elders

Thus, we reign.

LESSON 1:
THE KEY ELEMENTS OF THE COVENANT

> **Read through Deuteronomy 15:5-6 and write out the benefit of being in the Kingdom and experiencing Him reigning. (Who else gets to reign?)**
>
> ⁵ …if only you will strictly obey the voice of the Lord your God, being careful to do all this commandment that I command you today. ⁶ For the Lord your God will bless you, as he promised you, and you shall lend to many nations, but you shall not borrow, and you shall rule over many nations, but they shall not rule over you.

_____
_____
_____
_____
_____

Word Meanings: **Reign:** rule, have dominion, cause to rule, to exercise dominion

> **Read Romans 5:17.**
>
> ¹⁷ For if, because of one man's trespass, death reigned through that one man, much more will those who receive the abundance of grace and the free gift of righteousness reign in life through the one man Jesus Christ.

_____
_____
_____
_____
_____

    A wonderful benefit of being in His Kingdom under His reign is that we get to reign as well. This means we exercise the authority given to us in our circumstances and have dominion over circumstances and principalities and powers as so directed by God according to His Word and promises spoken to us. We only are able to receive this as we live in the Kingdom.

LESSON 1:
THE KEY ELEMENTS OF THE COVENANT

Word Meanings: **Abundance:** superabundantly, superiority, preference, pre-eminence, gain, profit, residue, remains: the wickedness remaining over in a Christian from his state prior to conversion

Reign: to be king, to exercise kingly power, to reign, of the governor of under his reign province, of the rule of the Messiah, of the reign of Christians in the millennium, to exercise the highest influence, to control

The covenant only operates in His Kingdom. We must be living in the Kingdom to experience the covenant. The covenant is not automatic. In other words, if we operate outside of the Kingdom, we will not be experiencing the covenant. There is a King who is on the throne, and that King reigns. If He reigns it means that we do not. We are to surrender our will to Him and abide with Him in order to be living in the Kingdom. It is a choice that we must make, and this choice is not permanent but rather moment by moment; and is why abiding is so critical to the process and is driven by our desire to live in the privilege of the covenant.

LESSON 2:
THE PRIVILEGES OF THE COVENANT

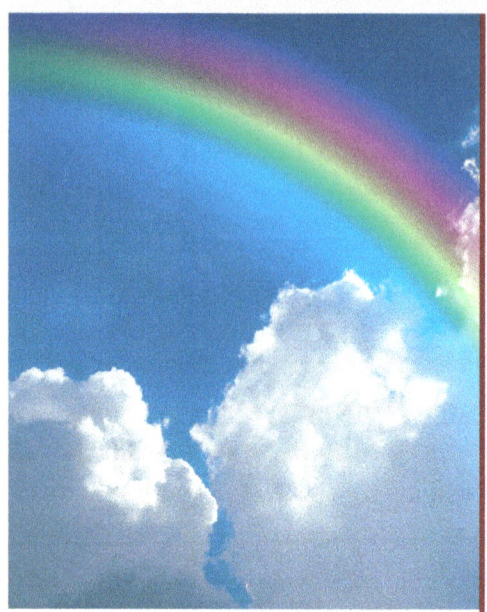

5. WHAT PRIVILEGES ARE WE GIVEN THROUGH THE COVENANT?

As you now move into this section, you will work through all of the specific benefits that are given to us as part of the covenant.

Protection/Safety/Enemies Defeated:

When we mention that we will receive protection, safety, and the defeat of our enemies, we know these are things we need because:

1. We have an enemy (Satan and the principalities and powers) and his ability to bring human enemies against us.

2. We are living in an unsafe world and will encounter trouble.

So, this does not mean we are taken out of these issues but rather that we will be given protection and victory when we do encounter the trouble and battles of life.

> "We can be assured that our enemies will be defeated, regardless of how strong they seem to be. Remember that the Lord will cause this."

Read through Deuteronomy 28:7 and write out those privileges that are promised as a recipient of the covenant? What do they mean to us today?

⁷ The Lord will cause your enemies who rise against you to be defeated before you. They shall come out against you one way and flee before you seven ways.

_____
_____
_____
_____
_____

LESSON 2:
THE PRIVILEGES OF THE COVENANT

We can be assured that our enemies will be defeated, regardless of how strong they seem to be. Remember that the Lord will cause this.

Word Meanings: **Arise:** stand, rise up, stand up
                                Flee: to escape, to take flight, depart, disappear

> **Read Psalm 91:1-16 and list all the benefits.**
>
> My Refuge and My Fortress
> **91** He who dwells in the shelter of the Most High
>   will abide in the shadow of the Almighty.
> ² I will say[a] to the Lord, "My refuge and my fortress,
>   my God, in whom I trust."
> ³ For he will deliver you from the snare of the fowler
>   and from the deadly pestilence.
> ⁴ He will cover you with his pinions,
>   and under his wings you will find refuge;
>   his faithfulness is a shield and buckler.
> ⁵ You will not fear the terror of the night,
>   nor the arrow that flies by day,
> ⁶ nor the pestilence that stalks in darkness,
>   nor the destruction that wastes at noonday.
> ⁷ A thousand may fall at your side,
>   ten thousand at your right hand,
>   but it will not come near you.
> ⁸ You will only look with your eyes
>   and see the recompense of the wicked.
> ⁹ Because you have made the Lord your dwelling place—
>   the Most High, who is my refuge[b]—
> ¹⁰ no evil shall be allowed to befall you,
>   no plague come near your tent.
> ¹¹ For he will command his angels concerning you
>   to guard you in all your ways.
> ¹² On their hands they will bear you up,
>   lest you strike your foot against a stone.
> ¹³ You will tread on the lion and the adder;
>   the young lion and the serpent you will trample underfoot.

LESSON 2:
THE PRIVILEGES OF THE COVENANT

> ¹⁴ "Because he holds fast to me in love, I will deliver him;
>   I will protect him, because he knows my name.
> ¹⁵ When he calls to me, I will answer him;
>   I will be with him in trouble;
>   I will rescue him and honor him.
> ¹⁶ With long life I will satisfy him
>   and show him my salvation."

_____
_____
_____
_____
_____
_____

This is what the Lord promises regarding protection and safety:
- Refuge
- Fortress
- Deliverance
- Shield
- Buckler
- Protection from arrows, pestilence, and destruction
- Our enemy will not come near us
- No evil will befall us (understand this does not mean trouble never comes our way but that the Hebrew words here mean that things that irritate, annoy, cause us frustration, etc. but will not characterize our life permanently. In other words, we do not need to put up with these difficult things as a way of life but expect God to take care of these things as we do encounter them. This is in line with what Jesus said in John 16:33, that in this life we will have trouble but are not to fret, He has overcome it)
- Angels will be in charge over us and protect us
- We will be delivered from trouble and be satisfied
- We will be given us specific answers to the troubles we are facing

LESSON 2:
THE PRIVILEGES OF THE COVENANT

Word Meanings: **Fortress:** stronghold
Refuge: shelter, from rain or storm, from danger, of falsehood
Deliver: to snatch away, deliver, rescue, save, strip, plunder
Snare: of calamities, plots, source or agent of calamity (*figuratively*); terror, dread
Evil: bad, evil (*adjective*), disagreeable, malignant, unpleasant, evil (*giving pain, unhappiness, misery*), displeasing, wicked (*ethically*), general, of persons, of thoughts, deeds, actions, distress, misery, injury, calamity (*noun masculine*), distress, adversity, befall
Meet: encounter, approach, be opportune
Be Satisfied: be sated, be fulfilled, be surfeited

Read Exodus 23:22-24.

²² But if you carefully obey his voice and do all that I say, then I will be an enemy to your enemies and an adversary to your adversaries.
²³ When my angel goes before you and brings you to the Amorites and the Hittites and the Perizzites and the Canaanites, the Hivites and the Jebusites, and I blot them out, ²⁴ you shall not bow down to their gods nor serve them, nor do as they do, but you shall utterly overthrow them and break their pillars in pieces.

_____
_____
_____
_____
_____

We can stand on the truth that God will actually be an adversary to our adversaries. Such an amazing power is available to us! We do not need to fight but our enemies will actually be fighting God, and He wins. Wow.

Word Meanings: **Be an Adversary:** treat as foe, show hostility to
Cut Off: to hide, conceal, cut down, make desolate, kick, to be hidden, to be effaced, be destroyed, be cut off

LESSON 2:
THE PRIVILEGES OF THE COVENANT

Goodness: His Good Treasure:

Goodness is the excellent, the best, the great life that God has planned out to give us. The world is one of steal, kill, and destroy and wants us to accept a life of mediocrity and constant failure. God assures us that although you will encounter trouble, His plan is for us to live in goodness—beauty, freedom, joy, peace—He is offering His best and none better.

> **Read Deuteronomy 28:11-12.**
>
> [11] And the Lord will make you abound in prosperity, in the fruit of your womb and in the fruit of your livestock and in the fruit of your ground, within the land that the Lord swore to your fathers to give you. [12] The Lord will open to you his good treasury, the heavens, to give the rain to your land in its season and to bless all the work of your hands. And you shall lend to many nations, but you shall not borrow.

_____
_____
_____
_____
_____

This is all about God's goodness—that which He determines to be excellent and beneficial to bless you. He says that He wants to bless the work of your hands to bring you income, bringing you both financial goodness, as well as an enjoyment for what you are doing. This will bring freedom, joy, and even positive material things, as these all are included in His ability to deliver positives into your life. Remember, it is always based on His definition and not ours, so we are not to compare what others might be receiving but rather the blessing that He so chooses for us.

Word Meanings: **Plenteous:** show excess, have more than enough, have an excess
Good: excellent (*of its kind*), rich, valuable in estimation, appropriate, becoming, better (*comparative*), glad, happy, prosperous (*of man's sensuous nature*), understanding (*of man's intellectual nature*), kind, benign, right (*ethical*), a good thing, benefit, welfare, prosperity, happiness
Treasure: storehouse

LESSON 2:
THE PRIVILEGES OF THE COVENANT

> **Read Psalm 25:9-14.**
>
> ⁹ He leads the humble in what is right,
>   and teaches the humble his way.
> ¹⁰ All the paths of the Lord are steadfast love and faithfulness,
>   for those who keep his covenant and his testimonies.
> ¹¹ For your name's sake, O Lord,
>   pardon my guilt, for it is great.
> ¹² Who is the man who fears the Lord?
>   Him will he instruct in the way that he should choose.
> ¹³ His soul shall abide in well-being,
>   and his offspring shall inherit the land.
> ¹⁴ The friendship[a] of the Lord is for those who fear him,
>   and he makes known to them his covenant.

_____
_____
_____
_____
_____

He describes what He promises to deliver as part of His goodness:

1. Show us the way He chooses for us
2. Prosperity
3. Secrets of special revelation to us
4. The deeper understanding of the covenant itself for us (blessed to be a blessing)

Word Meanings: **Covenant Loyalty:** goodness, kindness, faithfulness
Prosperity: excellent (*of its kind*), rich, valuable in estimation, appropriate, becoming, better (*comparative*), glad, happy, prosperous (*of man's sensuous nature*), understanding (**of man's intellectual nature**), kind, benign, right (*ethical*), a good thing, benefit, welfare, prosperity, happiness
Secret Counsel: familiar converse, intimacy

LESSON 2:
THE PRIVILEGES OF THE COVENANT

> **Read Psalm 85:10-13.**
>
> ¹⁰ Steadfast love and faithfulness meet;
>   righteousness and peace kiss each other.
> ¹¹ Faithfulness springs up from the ground,
>   and righteousness looks down from the sky.
> ¹² Yes, the Lord will give what is good,
>   and our land will yield its increase.
> ¹³ Righteousness will go before him
>   and make his footsteps a way.

_____
_____
_____
_____
_____

    Tied together that the Lord will give what is good (what has been explained above) to making His footsteps our pathway. Thus, as we walk in the Kingdom, He guarantees that His path is to bless us and give us what is good.

Word Meanings: **Peace/Shalom:** completeness, soundness, welfare, completeness (*in number*), safety, soundness (*in body*), welfare, health, prosperity, quiet, tranquility, contentment, friendship, of human relationships, with God especially in covenant relationship
Righteousness: justice, rightness, what is right or just or normal, justness
Truth: firmness, faithfulness, (*noun feminine*), sureness, reliability
Covenant Loyalty: goodness, kindness, faithfulness
Good: excellent (*of its kind*), rich, valuable in estimation, appropriate, becoming, better (*comparative*), glad, happy, prosperous (*of man's sensuous nature*), understanding (*of man's intellectual nature*), kind, benign, right (*ethical*), a good thing, benefit, welfare, prosperity, happiness

LESSON 2:
THE PRIVILEGES OF THE COVENANT

Peace:

Peace is shalom. It is not the absence of conflict but rather a much deeper understanding of how God defines this: abundant favor, prosperity, completeness, health. This broader definition is a significant part of the covenant promise. These verses each define an element of this deeper meaning:

> **Read Ezekiel 34:25.**
>
> The Lord's Covenant of Peace
> ^{25} "I will make with them a covenant of peace and banish wild beasts from the land, so that they may dwell securely in the wilderness and sleep in the woods."

_____
_____
_____
_____
_____

Safety/security: We are to live free of worry and anxiety.

Word Meanings: **Peace/Shalom:** completeness, soundness, welfare, completeness (*in number*), safety, soundness (*in body*), welfare, health, prosperity, quiet, tranquility, contentment, friendship, of human relationships, with God especially in covenant relationship
Safety: security, securely

> **Read Isaiah 54:10.**
>
> ^{10} For the mountains may depart
>   and the hills be removed,
> but my steadfast love shall not depart from you,
>   and my covenant of peace shall not be removed,"
>   says the Lord, who has compassion on you.

29

LESSON 2:
THE PRIVILEGES OF THE COVENANT

_____
_____
_____
_____
_____

We are to be assured that His covenant loyalty and shalom will always remain, and they are not arbitrary or limited.

Word Meanings: **Covenant Loyalty:** goodness, kindness, faithfulness
Peace/Shalom: completeness, soundness, welfare, completeness (*in number*), safety, soundness (*in body*), welfare, health, prosperity, quiet, tranquility, contentment, friendship, of human relationships, with God especially in covenant relationship

> **Read John 14:25-27.**
>
> [25] "These things I have spoken to you while I am still with you. [26] But the Helper, the Holy Spirit, whom the Father will send in my name, he will teach you all things and bring to your remembrance all that I have said to you. [27] Peace I leave with you; my peace I give to you. Not as the world gives do I give to you. Let not your hearts be troubled, neither let them be afraid.

_____
_____
_____
_____
_____

He is our peace, and it is given to us regardless of circumstances. We live in Him—in the covenant—so our peace is not dependent upon circumstances. It comes from being in Him, and thus we are not to allow troubling things to draw us out of this place of peace.

LESSON 2:
THE PRIVILEGES OF THE COVENANT

Word Meanings: **Peace/Shalom:** completeness, soundness, welfare, completeness (*in number*), safety, soundness (*in body*), welfare, health, prosperity, quiet, tranquility, contentment, friendship, of human relationships, with God especially in covenant relationship

Give: to give something to someone; of one's own accord to give one something, to his advantage, to bestow a gift, to grant, give to one asking, let have, to supply, furnish, necessary things

> **Read John 16:33.**
>
> ³³ I have said these things to you, that in me you may have peace. In the world you will have tribulation. But take heart; I have overcome the world."

_____
_____
_____
_____
_____

Yes, in the world we will have trouble, so we are not to think that life in shalom is absent of trouble, but He promises to get us out of any trouble, so we can always stay in peace. His favor will be characteristic of our life, and we can count on it because He has overcome the world, and the covenant life is a life of overcoming.

Word Meanings: **Peace/Shalom:** completeness, soundness, welfare, completeness (*in number*), safety, soundness (*in body*), welfare, health, prosperity, quiet, tranquility, contentment, friendship, of human relationships, with God especially in covenant relationship

Trouble: a pressing, pressing together, pressure, oppression, affliction, tribulation, distress, straits

Overcome: to conquer; to carry off the victory, come off victorious, of Christ, victorious over all His foes

LESSON 2:
THE PRIVILEGES OF THE COVENANT

Abundance:

Abundance contrasts the difference between God's best with mediocrity. The covenant will be giving us things that are excellent and superb and wonderful versus average or something by which we barely get by. Realize this high standard and never accept mediocrity.

Read Deuteronomy 28:1-14 and list all blessings.

Blessings for Obedience
28 "And if you faithfully obey the voice of the Lord your God, being careful to do all his commandments that I command you today, the Lord your God will set you high above all the nations of the earth. ² And all these blessings shall come upon you and overtake you, if you obey the voice of the Lord your God. ³ Blessed shall you be in the city and blessed shall you be in the field. ⁴ Blessed shall be the fruit of your womb and the fruit of your ground and the fruit of your cattle, the increase of your herds and the young of your flock. ⁵ Blessed shall be your basket and your kneading bowl. ⁶ Blessed shall you be when you come in and blessed shall you be when you go out.

⁷ "The Lord will cause your enemies who rise against you to be defeated before you. They shall come out against you one way and flee before you seven ways. ⁸ The Lord will command the blessing on you in your barns and in all that you undertake. And he will bless you in the land that the Lord your God is giving you. ⁹ The Lord will establish you as a people holy to himself, as he has sworn to you, if you keep the commandments of the Lord your God and walk in his ways. ¹⁰ And all the peoples of the earth shall see that you are called by the name of the Lord, and they shall be afraid of you. ¹¹ And the Lord will make you abound in prosperity, in the fruit of your womb and in the fruit of your livestock and in the fruit of your ground, within the land that the Lord swore to your fathers to give you. ¹² The Lord will open to you his good treasury, the heavens, to give the rain to your land in its season and to bless all the work of your hands. And you shall lend to many nations, but you shall not borrow. ¹³ And the Lord will make you the head and not the tail, and you shall only go up and not down, if you obey the commandments of the Lord your God, which I command you today, being careful to do them, ¹⁴ and if you do not turn aside from any of the words that I command you today, to the right hand or to the left, to go after other gods to serve them.

LESSON 2:
THE PRIVILEGES OF THE COVENANT

_____
_____
_____
_____
_____

All the aspects of these verses detail those promises of the covenant life as they define what abundant blessings truly are:

- In city and country (wherever you live and go)
- Your livelihood
- Your provision
- Your going in and going out (your everyday life)
- The defeat of your enemies
- The command of your storehouses to be blessed (meaning you will have plenty without living hand to mouth)
- Live a holy life (be transformed and life in freedom)
- Work be blessed (joy and success)
- Be the head and not the tail (have authority)

Word Meanings: **Kneading Trough or Bowl:** store, what remains, is extra
Put Your Hand: undertaking (*that to which one stretches out the hand*), place of letting or turning loose
To Be Opened: be let loose, be thrown open

Read Deuteronomy 6:1-3.

The Greatest Commandment
6 "Now this is the commandment—the statutes and the rules[a]—that the Lord your God commanded me to teach you, that you may do them in the land to which you are going over, to possess it, ² that you may fear the Lord your God, you and your son and your son's son, by keeping all his statutes and his commandments, which I command you, all the days of your life, and that your days may be long.³ Hear therefore, O Israel, and be careful to do them, that it may go well with you, and that you may multiply greatly, as the Lord, the God of your fathers, has promised you, in a land flowing with milk and honey.

LESSON 2:
THE PRIVILEGES OF THE COVENANT

_____
_____
_____
_____
_____

Life will go well—a joy and pleasing—beautiful by nature (remember, this does not mean life will be free of trouble but instead one characterized by things going well because He makes things go well).

Word Meanings: **Be Well:** be good, be pleasing, be glad, to be glad, be joyful, to be well placed, to be well for, be well with, go well with, to be pleasing, be pleasing to, to make glad, rejoice, to do good to, deal well with, to do well, do thoroughly or make a thing good or right or beautiful, do right
Mightily: exceedingly, much (*adverb*), might, force, abundance (*substantive*), muchness, force, abundance, exceedingly (*noun masculine*)
Increase: become great

Read Genesis 39:5-6.

⁵ From the time that he made him overseer in his house and over all that he had, the Lord blessed the Egyptian's house for Joseph's sake; the blessing of the Lord was on all that he had, in house and field. ⁶ So he left all that he had in Joseph's charge, and because of him he had no concern about anything but the food he ate.

Now Joseph was handsome in form and appearance.

_____
_____
_____
_____
_____

LESSON 2:
THE PRIVILEGES OF THE COVENANT

Everything and everyone around you will also be blessed—not because of them but because of you and you living in the covenant. They just have to receive and honor you (part of being blessed because they bless you).

Word Meanings: **Blessing:** prosperity, praise of God; hand of: strength, power (*figuratively*)
Favored: to see, observe, consider, look at, give attention to, discern, distinguish

LESSON 3:
THE PRIVILEGES OF THE COVENANT (CON'T)

As in Lesson 2, continue to read through each set of verses writing out the privileges that are promised as a recipient of the covenant. What do they mean to us today?

Restoration:

Many who are beginning to understand the covenant are in places where they have lost things, ruined things, experienced difficulty and hardship. They wonder if the covenant still applies now, from this place of loss and ruin? The answer is an emphatic "YES" and is a critical part of the covenant life. It is from now forward. How about now?

Read Ezekiel 36:33-36.

33 "Thus says the Lord God: On the day that I cleanse you from all your iniquities, I will cause the cities to be inhabited, and the waste places shall be rebuilt. 34 And the land that was desolate shall be tilled, instead of being the desolation that it was in the sight of all who passed by. 35 And they will say, 'This land that was desolate has become like the garden of Eden, and the waste and desolate and ruined cities are now fortified and inhabited.' 36 Then the nations that are left all around you shall know that I am the Lord; I have rebuilt the ruined places and replanted that which was desolate. I am the Lord; I have spoken, and I will do it.

> "Many who are beginning to understand the covenant are in places where they have lost things, ruined things, experienced difficulty and hardship."

_____
_____
_____
_____
_____
_____
_____

LESSON 3:
THE PRIVILEGES OF THE COVENANT (CON'T)

He promises that what has been laid to waste and ruined (usually by our own doing when we choose not to walk in the covenant—although it matters not as we are always invited from now forward to walk in the covenant), will be restored to the qualities of the garden, which is what we are describing in all these benefits (the Garden of Eden). It is His work, and He will deliver this through the covenant. Notice that the rebuilding process does take time. It is a step-by-step process, but it will be delivered.

Word Meanings:

Waste: place laid waste, ruin, desolation
Rebuilt: to be rebuilt, established (*of restored exiles*) (*figuratively*), established (*made permanent*)
Desolated: be deflowered, be deserted, be appalled
Garden: enclosed garden (*figuratively of a bride*)

Read Psalm 40:1-3.

My Help and My Deliverer
To the choirmaster. A Psalm of David.
40 I waited patiently for the Lord;
 he inclined to me and heard my cry.
² He drew me up from the pit of destruction,
 out of the miry bog,
and set my feet upon a rock,
 making my steps secure.
³ He put a new song in my mouth,
 a song of praise to our God.
Many will see and fear,
 and put their trust in the Lord.

_____
_____
_____
_____
_____

LESSON 3:
THE PRIVILEGES OF THE COVENANT (CON'T)

This describes a situation where we are literally stuck in the mud and have no way of finding a resolution on our own. We see, though, that He will literally move us out of this awful situation and place us back out of trouble and onto a solid foundation where our steps will be reestablished in the covenant life. We will then rejoice because of it.

Word Meanings:

Brought Up: be taken up, be brought up, be taken away
Set: to be firm, be stable, be established, to be set up, be established, be fixed
Rock: as stronghold of Jehovah, of security

Read Joel 2:21-27.

[21] "Fear not, O land;
  be glad and rejoice,
   for the Lord has done great things!
[22] Fear not, you beasts of the field,
   for the pastures of the wilderness are green;
the tree bears its fruit;
   the fig tree and vine give their full yield.
[23] "Be glad, O children of Zion,
   and rejoice in the Lord your God,
for he has given the early rain for your vindication;
   he has poured down for you abundant rain,
   the early and the latter rain, as before.
[24] "The threshing floors shall be full of grain;
   the vats shall overflow with wine and oil.
[25] I will restore[a] to you the years
   that the swarming locust has eaten,
the hopper, the destroyer, and the cutter,
   my great army, which I sent among you.
[26] "You shall eat in plenty and be satisfied,
   and praise the name of the Lord your God,
   who has dealt wondrously with you.
And my people shall never again be put to shame.
[27] You shall know that I am in the midst of Israel,
   and that I am the Lord your God and there is none else.
And my people shall never again be put to shame.

LESSON 3:
THE PRIVILEGES OF THE COVENANT (CON'T)

_____
_____
_____
_____
_____

God will restore to us completely that which has been lost. In His economy, it doesn't matter how deep the trouble or how much time has passed. He is fully able to restore our lives completely to the fullness of the covenant now. We are assured in the fullness of the gospel that nothing is too difficult for Him and that restoration can be complete and wonderful as we now experience the covenant life.

Word Meanings: **Restore:** to cause to be at peace, to live in peace, to be complete, be sound, be finished, be ended, to be sound, be uninjured, to complete, finish, to make safe, to make whole or good, restore, make compensation, to make good, pay, to requite, recompense, reward, to be performed, to be repaid, be requited, perform
To Be Satisfied: be sated, be fulfilled, be surfeited
Wondrously: to be marvelous, be wonderful, be surpassing, be extraordinary, separate by distinguishing action

Wisdom and Knowledge:

One of the great privileges of living in the covenant is receiving the wisdom and knowledge of God—and seeing things as God sees them. This is not just from the natural world, which is limited, but from the spiritual and from many dimensions. This will give us insight as to what His greater purposes are, that which He wishes to fulfill and do, and how He wants us to step along the path. We then will trust our steps because we can be confident that He knows what's ahead and around the corner—which we do not.

> **Read 2 Chronicles 1:9-12.**
>
> [9] O Lord God, let your word to David my father be now fulfilled, for you have made me king over a people as numerous as the dust of the earth. [10] Give me now wisdom and knowledge to go out and come in before this people, for who can govern this people of yours, which is so great?" [11] God answered Solomon, "Because this was in your heart, and you have not asked for possessions, wealth, honor, or the life of those who hate you, and have not even asked for long life, but have asked for

LESSON 3:
THE PRIVILEGES OF THE COVENANT (CON'T)

> *wisdom and knowledge for yourself that you may govern my people over whom I have made you king,* ¹² *wisdom and knowledge are granted to you. I will also give you riches, possessions, and honor, such as none of the kings had who were before you, and none after you shall have the like."*

_____
_____
_____
_____
_____

    As part of His loyalty to the covenant, He promises to give us this wisdom and knowledge in order that we might have discernment. Why? In order to perceive and understand what we would consider good and God's best, we need His wisdom—wisdom He offers through His covenant. God can see the future and what is around the corner; and knows what will bring us good and what would bring us things that would be difficult and troublesome.

Word Meanings: **Covenant Loyalty:** goodness, kindness, faithfulness
Knowledge: mind, thought, perceive and see, find out and discern
Wisdom: skill (*in war*), in administration, shrewdness, prudence (*in religious affairs*), ethical and religious

> **Read 1 Corinthians 1:30.**
>
> ³⁰ And because of him[a] you are in Christ Jesus, who became to us wisdom from God, righteousness and sanctification and redemption…

_____
_____
_____
_____
_____

LESSON 3:
THE PRIVILEGES OF THE COVENANT (CON'T)

Christ is wisdom; and because we have the Holy Spirit, we have all wisdom. Walking in the Kingdom means we have access to all wisdom and nothing will be beyond our reach—the grand privilege of being in the covenant.

Word Meanings: **Wisdom:** broad and full of intelligence; used of the knowledge of very diverse matters, the wisdom, which belongs to men, specifically the varied knowledge of things human and divine, acquired by acuteness and experience, and summed up in maxims and proverbs, the science and learning, the act of interpreting dreams and always giving the sagest advice, the intelligence evinced in discovering the meaning of some mysterious number or vision skill in the management of affairs, devout and proper prudence in intercourse with men not disciples of Christ, skill and discretion in imparting Christian truth, the knowledge and practice of the requisites for godly and upright living

Establish in Us Good Works:

Our good works will be strictly the assignments given by Him. They are not what we determine are good ideas or worthwhile acts of service, but rather any work that He has called us to. This is to be carried out day by day and not looked at as programs or ministries; so, it can include taking a vacation or time of recreation, taking time with a grandchild, spending time with our spouse, etc. How ever He wishes us to spend our day, this is His good work for the "now." It will include our vocation and our ministry work but is not exclusive of those. Remember that all of that is not of our choosing but instead His assignments for us—and within those assignments are specific activities that He designates for the now. They are His plan, not ours.

> **Read 2 Thessalonians 2:16.**
>
> ¹⁶ Now may our Lord Jesus Christ himself, and God our Father, who loved us and gave us eternal comfort and good hope through grace…

_____
_____
_____
_____
_____

LESSON 3:
THE PRIVILEGES OF THE COVENANT (CON'T)

He establishes the good work. We don't.

Word Meanings: **Good:** good constitution or nature, useful, salutary, pleasant, agreeable, joyful, happy, excellent, distinguished, upright, honorable

> **Read Hebrews 13:20-21.**
>
> Benediction
> [20] Now may the God of peace who brought again from the dead our Lord Jesus, the great shepherd of the sheep, by the blood of the eternal covenant, [21] equip you with everything good that you may do his will, working in us[a] that which is pleasing in his sight, through Jesus Christ, to whom be glory forever and ever. Amen.

_____
_____
_____
_____
_____

He ordains what is His will. These are pleasing to Him, according to His purposes and are part of a bigger story that we are joining (and according to His covenant plan). Through our joining Him in this, we are made complete—whole, transformed, and full of the blessings He has ordained.

Word Meanings: **Equip:** fit out, put in order, arrange, adjust, to fit or frame for one's self, prepare, ethically: to strengthen, perfect, complete, make one what he ought to be
Good: good constitution or nature, useful, salutary, pleasant, agreeable, joyful, happy, excellent, distinguished, upright, honorable
Work: produce, construct, form, fashion

Covenant/Promise(s):

Inherent in the covenant, which is that we will be given blessings (in order to be a blessing), we will be given promises. These are Rhema words that are specifically given to us and that are unique to us.

LESSON 3:
THE PRIVILEGES OF THE COVENANT (CON'T)

> **Read Galatians 3:10-18, 3:26-29.**
>
> The Righteous Shall Live by Faith
> [10] For all who rely on works of the law are under a curse; for it is written, "Cursed be everyone who does not abide by all things written in the Book of the Law, and do them." [11] Now it is evident that no one is justified before God by the law, for "The righteous shall live by faith."[a] [12] But the law is not of faith, rather "The one who does them shall live by them." [13] Christ redeemed us from the curse of the law by becoming a curse for us—for it is written, "Cursed is everyone who is hanged on a tree"— [14] so that in Christ Jesus the blessing of Abraham might come to the Gentiles, so that we might receive the promised Spirit[b] through faith.
>
> The Law and the Promise
> [15] To give a human example, brothers:[c] even with a man-made covenant, no one annuls it or adds to it once it has been ratified. [16] Now the promises were made to Abraham and to his offspring. It does not say, "And to offsprings," referring to many, but referring to one, "And to your offspring," who is Christ. [17] This is what I mean: the law, which came 430 years afterward, does not annul a covenant previously ratified by God, so as to make the promise void. [18] For if the inheritance comes by the law, it no longer comes by promise; but God gave it to Abraham by a promise.
>
> [26] for in Christ Jesus you are all sons of God, through faith. [27] For as many of you as were baptized into Christ have put on Christ. [28] There is neither Jew nor Greek, there is neither slave[a] nor free, there is no male and female, for you are all one in Christ Jesus. [29] And if you are Christ's, then you are Abraham's offspring, heirs according to promise.

_____
_____
_____
_____
_____

    This discussion in Galatians states that these promises our available only if we are living and walking in Christ (which is why we need to be in the Kingdom where the covenant is delivered). Why? Because the promise(s) is only given to Christ as the heir to the covenant of Abraham and not to heirs. This means we are not the

LESSON 3:
THE PRIVILEGES OF THE COVENANT (CON'T)

sole recipients of the promise(s) of the covenant, as only Christ is the sole recipient and heir. But, we then can be recipients of the promise(s) as we so walk in and live in Christ, because He then transfers these to us who are co-heirs with Him. This, then, is why we cannot name it and claim it nor just expect to receive it because we are a child of God. Rather, we must be in Christ and then receive what He so speaks and gives us as His promise(s) to us. This is why we are called to be in His Kingdom and let Him be the King and not us. We will be recipients as part of the covenant since giving promises is part and partial to His nature and the essence of the covenant. It is how things are delivered uniquely to our path and live in our unique circumstances.

Word Meanings:

Promise: the act of promising, a promise given or to be given, a promised good or blessing

Confirmed: to sanction, ratify, or establish beforehand

Heir: one who receives by lot, an heir, in Messianic usage, one who receives his allotted possession by right of sonship, one who has acquired or obtained the portion allotted to him

---

What Does He Promise?
Read Psalm 111:5-9.

⁵ He provides food for those who fear him;
　he remembers his covenant forever.
⁶ He has shown his people the power of his works,
　in giving them the inheritance of the nations.
⁷ The works of his hands are faithful and just;
　all his precepts are trustworthy;
⁸ they are established forever and ever,
　to be performed with faithfulness and uprightness.
⁹ He sent redemption to his people;
　he has commanded his covenant forever.
　Holy and awesome is his name!

_____
_____
_____
_____
_____

LESSON 3:
THE PRIVILEGES OF THE COVENANT (CON'T)

God promises to be mindful of His loyalty to the covenant and to command His promises forever. They will be given, we can be assured, and they will stand fast.

Word Meanings: **Power:** strength, might, human strength, strength (*of angels*), power (*of God*), strength (*of animals*), produce, wealth (*of soil*)
Truth: sureness, reliability, stability, continuance, faithfulness, as spoken, of testimony and judgment, of divine instruction, truth as a body of ethical or religious knowledge, true doctrine
Good: good constitution or nature, useful, salutary, pleasant, agreeable, joyful, happy, excellent, distinguished, upright, honorable
Understanding: prudence, insight

> **Read Psalm 23:6.**
>
> 6 Surely[a] goodness and mercy[b] shall follow me
>   all the days of my life,
> and I shall dwell[c] in the house of the Lord
>   forever.[d]

_____
_____
_____
_____
_____

His covenant loyalty will follow us all the days of our lives—not sometimes but always.

Word Meanings: **Goodness:** good constitution or nature, useful, salutary, pleasant, agreeable, joyful, happy, excellent, distinguished, upright, honorable
Mercy: covenant loyalty
Follow: to be behind, follow after, pursue

> **Read 1 Thessalonians 5:24.**
>
> 24 He who calls you is faithful; he will surely do it.

LESSON 3:
THE PRIVILEGES OF THE COVENANT (CON'T)

_____
_____
_____
_____
_____

    We can be assured that what He does promise, He will perform and complete. It will happen in reality and our circumstances will change. As we live in the covenant, our blessings will be real and wonderful.

Word Meanings: **Faithful:** trusty, of persons who show themselves faithful in the transaction of business, the execution of commands, or the discharge of official duties, one who kept his plighted faith, worthy of trust, that can be relied on

Perform It: to make, with the names of things made, to produce, construct, form, fashion, etc., to be the authors of, the cause, to make ready, to prepare, bear, shoot forth, to acquire, to provide a thing for one's self, to make a thing out of something

Commands Blessing:

    He wants us to understand that the covenant will be a life of Him commanding blessing (it will happen), which we can count on, and not wonder if it will happen. It will because it will be commanded.

Read Deuteronomy 28:8.

⁸ The Lord will command the blessing on you in your barns and in all that you undertake. And he will bless you in the land that the Lord your God is giving you.

_____
_____
_____
_____
_____

LESSON 3:
THE PRIVILEGES OF THE COVENANT (CON'T)

When God commands the promises, we can be assured that they will absolutely happen, because He is not merely giving some random suggestion. When He commands something, it will be so. Why? Because He has the power and might to make it happen. He is sovereign, nothing is too difficult for Him, and all things are possible.

Word Meanings: **Command:** charge, give orders, lay charge, give charge to, order

> **Read Psalm 133:1-3.**
>
> When Brothers Dwell in Unity
> A Song of Ascents. Of David.
> **133** Behold, how good and pleasant it is
>   when brothers dwell in unity![a]
> ² It is like the precious oil on the head,
>   running down on the beard,
> on the beard of Aaron,
>   running down on the collar of his robes!
> ³ It is like the dew of Hermon,
>   which falls on the mountains of Zion!
> For there the Lord has commanded the blessing,
>   life forevermore.

_____
_____
_____
_____

Here we see another statement where He commands blessing. It will happen. We will discuss the condition of unity later, but for now understand that when He commands blessing, it will be so.

Good: good constitution or nature, useful, salutary, pleasant, agreeable, joyful, happy, excellent, distinguished, upright, honorable
Pleasant: delightful, sweet, lovely, agreeable
Delightful: lovely, beautiful

LESSON 4:
OUR RESPONSIBILITIES IN THIS AGREEMENT

6. WHAT ARE OUR RESPONSIBILITIES IN THE AGREEMENT?

Now that we have discussed the benefits of the covenant, and we have an understanding that a covenant is an agreement where both sides have responsibility for the agreement, we now will discuss what those responsibilities are.

Do What Is Right and Hate Evil:

Our first call is to follow God's instructions and do what we know is right in His eyes. This means we are to rid our lives of anything that is not pleasing to God or takes away the power of the life of God.

Read through the following verses in Chronicles noting those actions of the kings who were deemed "good and right in the eyes of the Lord." How would we translate these into what would be good and right in the eyes of the Lord in our lives? What specifically is God asking you to do that is good and right, right now?

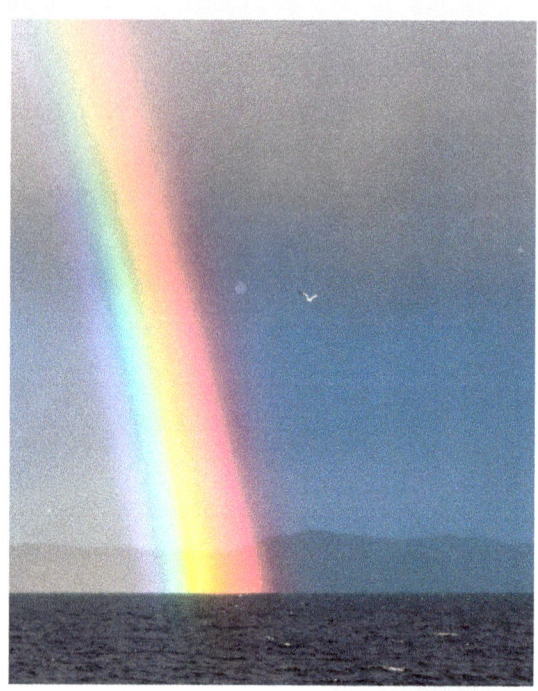

> "Our first call is to follow God's instructions and do what we know is right in His eyes."

Read 2 Chronicles 14:2-6, 26:4-5, 31:20-21.

2 [a] And Asa did what was good and right in the eyes of the Lord his God. 3 He took away the foreign altars and the high places and broke down the pillars and cut down the Asherim 4 and commanded Judah to seek the Lord, the God of their fathers, and to keep the law and the commandment. 5 He also took out of all the cities of Judah the high places and the incense altars. And the kingdom had rest under him. 6 He built fortified cities in Judah, for the land had rest. He had no war in those years, for the Lord gave him peace.

4 And he did what was right in the eyes of the Lord, according to all that his father Amaziah had done. 5 He set himself to seek God in the days of Zechariah, who instructed him in the fear of God, and as long as he sought the Lord, God made him prosper.

LESSON 4:
OUR RESPONSIBILITIES IN THIS AGREEMENT

> [20] Thus Hezekiah did throughout all Judah, and he did what was good and right and faithful before the Lord his God. [21] And every work that he undertook in the service of the house of God and in accordance with the law and the commandments, seeking his God, he did with all his heart, and prospered.

_____
_____
_____
_____
_____

These are the actions of Asa, Uzziah, and Hezekiah that were defined as good and right in the eyes of the Lord His God:

1. Asa removed altars to foreign gods and high places (anything that was more important in our lives than God), broke down sacred pillars and cut down wooden images, and commanded everyone to seek the Lord and follow God's instructions.

2. Uzziah sought God in everything.

3. Hezekiah sought the Lord and did everything for God with all his heart.

Word Meanings:

Right: pleasing, correct, straightforward, just, upright, fitting, proper
Good: good constitution or nature, useful, salutary, pleasant, agreeable, joyful, happy, excellent, distinguished, upright, honorable
Break In or Down: rend violently, wreck, crush, quench
Took Away: to be removed, to come to an end
Image: idol, used in idolatrous worship
Quiet: be tranquil, be at peace, be quiet, rest, lie still, be undisturbed
Rest: same as quiet
Build: rebuild, establish, cause to continue
Sought: to resort to, seek, seek with care, enquire, require
Understand: consider, to perceive, discern
Prosper: to advance, make progress, succeed, be profitable

LESSON 4:
OUR RESPONSIBILITIES IN THIS AGREEMENT

> **Read through Philippians 1:27-30 and note what it means to be worthy of walking of the Gospel. What does that mean to you, and how might God be calling you to adjust your life right now?**
>
> [27] Only let your manner of life be worthy[a] of the gospel of Christ, so that whether I come and see you or am absent, I may hear of you that you are standing firm in one spirit, with one mind striving side by side for the faith of the gospel, [28] and not frightened in anything by your opponents. This is a clear sign to them of their destruction, but of your salvation, and that from God. [29] For it has been granted to you that for the sake of Christ you should not only believe in him but also suffer for his sake, [30] engaged in the same conflict that you saw I had and now hear that I still have.

_____
_____
_____
_____
_____

    We are to live out our lives worthy of the Gospel by standing fast together in one Spirit, seeking together to walk in unity of the Spirit (knowing God's will), and not being terrified of the enemy but knowing that the covenant life stands, and together we will be blessed to be a blessing.

Word Meanings:

Worthy: suitably, worthily, in a manner worthy of weighing, having weight, having the weight of another thing of like value, worth as much, befitting, congruous, corresponding to a thing

To Strive Together: at the same time with another

Opposing: to be set over against, opposite to, to oppose, be averse to, withstand

LESSON 4:
OUR RESPONSIBILITIES IN THIS AGREEMENT

> **Read through Matthew 10:34-39 and note how Jesus defines who is worthy of following Him. What does that mean for you, and how He is calling you to respond to Him right now?**
>
> Not Peace, but a Sword
> ³⁴ "Do not think that I have come to bring peace to the earth. I have not come to bring peace, but a sword. ³⁵ For I have come to set a man against his father, and a daughter against her mother, and a daughter-in-law against her mother-in-law.³⁶ And a person's enemies will be those of his own household. ³⁷ Whoever loves father or mother more than me is not worthy of me, and whoever loves son or daughter more than me is not worthy of me. ³⁸ And whoever does not take his cross and follow me is not worthy of me. ³⁹ Whoever finds his life will lose it, and whoever loses his life for my sake will find it.

_____

_____

_____

_____

_____

    How do we know who is worthy? This is simply anyone who has a heart to live in the covenant. This means those who live in the Kingdom, who put the King above everything else, including each other, and even those close to us. This is an important truth to hammer home: Our allegiance is first and foremost to Christ. To live in the covenant means that He must truly be King, and we must surrender to Him being King. If not, we will be in the flesh and cannot participate in the Kingdom and are outside of the covenant.

Word Meanings: **At Variance:** cut into two parts, cleave asunder, sever
Above: on behalf of, for the sake of, over, beyond, more than, more
Worthy: suitably, worthily, in a manner worthy of weighing, having weight, having the weight of another thing of like value, worth as much, befitting, congruous, corresponding to a thing
Take: to take with the hand, lay hold of any person or thing in order to use it, to take up a thing to be carried, to take upon one's self, to take in order to carry away

LESSON 4:
OUR RESPONSIBILITIES IN THIS AGREEMENT

The Cross: not my cross
Follow: one who precedes, join him as his attendant, accompany him, to join one as a disciple, become or be his disciple
Lose: to destroy, to put out of the way entirely, abolish, put an end to, ruin, render useless

Be Separate:

We must understand what being separate really is all about: Jesus has not taken us out of the world nor has He asked us to completely separate from the world per se. This discussion is about being separate from influences that would dominate or have decision-making control over us: our closest friendships, advisers, partnerships, inner circle, etc. So, this is not about having relationships with unbelievers (we are called to spread the good news) but rather about who we spend most of our time with, namely our inner circle.

> **Read through Psalm 1:1 and write out what this verse says about how we are to respond to those who are not willing to walk with God.**
>
> The Way of the Righteous and the Wicked
> **1** Blessed is the man[a]
>   who walks not in the counsel of the wicked,
> nor stands in the way of sinners,
>   nor sits in the seat of scoffers.

_____
_____
_____
_____
_____

It is clear that we are not to receive the counsel of or be sitting with those who are ungodly, those who do not have a heart to follow God, or those who refuse to walk in the covenant and thus not seek together His Kingdom nor His will. Our closest friends are those who are going to be living out the covenant with us, and no one else.

LESSON 4:
OUR RESPONSIBILITIES IN THIS AGREEMENT

Word Meanings:
Scorn: make mouths at, talk arrogantly, mock, deride
Sinners: sinful, exposed to condemnation, reckoned as offenders

> **Read through 2 Corinthians 6:11-18 and note the truth about those relationships that reside in the darkness. What does that mean about relating to unbelievers/those who are not walking with God versus being in partnership and yoked to unbelievers/those who are not walking with God? What is the difference, and why is this so important to our life with God?**
>
> 11 We have spoken freely to you,[a] Corinthians; our heart is wide open. 12 You are not restricted by us, but you are restricted in your own affections. 13 In return (I speak as to children) widen your hearts also.
>
> The Temple of the Living God
> 14 Do not be unequally yoked with unbelievers. For what partnership has righteousness with lawlessness? Or what fellowship has light with darkness? 15 What accord has Christ with Belial?[b] Or what portion does a believer share with an unbeliever? 16 What agreement has the temple of God with idols? For we are the temple of the living God; as God said,
>
> "I will make my dwelling among them and walk among them,
> and I will be their God,
>   and they shall be my people.
> 17 Therefore go out from their midst,
>   and be separate from them, says the Lord,
> and touch no unclean thing;
>   then I will welcome you,
> 18 and I will be a father to you,
>   and you shall be sons and daughters to me,
> says the Lord Almighty."

_____
_____
_____
_____
_____

LESSON 4:
OUR RESPONSIBILITIES IN THIS AGREEMENT

Righteousness cannot be with lawlessness, light cannot be with darkness, Christ cannot be with evil, believers (faithful) cannot be with unbelievers (no faith), the godly cannot be with idols. The basic principle of living in the covenant means we cannot have holiness living with un-holiness. This is another truth as to why the covenant only operates in the Kingdom of God. And why we are to separate ourselves from un-holiness, as this is a fundamental spiritual principle that is critical to us operating in the Kingdom and in the covenant. Thus, we are not to be in partnership with, or allied to, any relationship where darkness (un-godliness) can control or influence us to counter God's will or walk with God into His covenant life.

Word Meanings:

Unequally Yoked: come under an unequal or different yoke, to be unequally yoked, to have fellowship with one who is not an equal: 2 Corinthians 6:14, where the apostle is forbidding Christians to have intercourse with idolaters

Partnership: a sharing, communion, fellowship

Lawlessness: contempt and violation of law, iniquity, wickedness

Darkness: of ignorance respecting divine things and human duties, and the accompanying ungodliness and immorality, together with their consequent misery in hell, persons in whom darkness becomes visible and holds sway

Harmony: concord, agreement

Agreement: a putting together or joint deposit (of votes), hence approval, assent

---

Read through 1 Corinthians 15:33-34 and write out the impact that the ungodly can have on us if we spend too much time in relationship with them as a normal way of life? Why is this so important as to how we then live in our walk with God?

[33] Do not be deceived: "Bad company ruins good morals."[a] [34] Wake up from your drunken stupor, as is right, and do not go on sinning. For some have no knowledge of God. I say this to your shame.

_____
_____
_____
_____
_____

LESSON 4:
OUR RESPONSIBILITIES IN THIS AGREEMENT

Another truth that we should recognize is that evil (ungodly) company (who we might have influence us) will corrupt us. We must be careful about whom we have as advisers and who we allow to influence us. We are to be around unbelievers and sinners to help them see the life and love of Christ, but we are not to spend primary time around those who will negatively influence us.

Word Meanings: **Corrupt:** to destroy; in the opinion of the Jews, the temple was corrupted or "destroyed" when anyone defiled or in the slightest degree damaged anything in it, or if its guardians neglected their duties, to lead away a Christian church from that state of knowledge and holiness in which it ought to abide
Bad: nature not such as it ought to be, of a mode of thinking, feeling, acting, base, wrong, wicked, troublesome, injurious, pernicious, destructive, baneful
Ignorance: not knowing

Obedience/Faithfulness:

As God gives us promises, He will give us instruction regarding the steps of following His will to receive these promises, and these will be delivered supernaturally. He needs to move us to the right place, at the right time, with the right people for Him to fulfill His purposes and thus His grand plan and the privilege for us to experience His wonderful promises to us. Our role is then to follow His instruction, to be obedient to what He tells us.

> **Read through Deuteronomy 28:1-2 and write out the conditions to receiving the blessings promised in the covenant. What does that mean is critical to us in the process?**
>
> Blessings for Obedience
> **28** "And if you faithfully obey the voice of the Lord your God, being careful to do all his commandments that I command you today, the Lord your God will set you high above all the nations of the earth. ² And all these blessings shall come upon you and overtake you, if you obey the voice of the Lord your God.

_____
_____
_____
_____

LESSON 4:
OUR RESPONSIBILITIES IN THIS AGREEMENT

Word Meanings: **Hear:** listen to, obey, to hear (*perceive by ear*), to hear of or concerning, hear (*have power to hear*), to hear with attention or interest, to understand
Observe: to keep, guard, observe, give heed, have charge of, keep watch and ward, protect, save life
Overtake: take hold upon

Read Deuteronomy 30:9-20.

⁹ The Lord your God will make you abundantly prosperous in all the work of your hand, in the fruit of your womb and in the fruit of your cattle and in the fruit of your ground. For the Lord will again take delight in prospering you, as he took delight in your fathers, ¹⁰ when you obey the voice of the Lord your God, to keep his commandments and his statutes that are written in this Book of the Law, when you turn to the Lord your God with all your heart and with all your soul.

The Choice of Life and Death
¹¹ "For this commandment that I command you today is not too hard for you, neither is it far off. ¹² It is not in heaven, that you should say, 'Who will ascend to heaven for us and bring it to us, that we may hear it and do it?' ¹³ Neither is it beyond the sea, that you should say, 'Who will go over the sea for us and bring it to us, that we may hear it and do it?' ¹⁴ But the word is very near you. It is in your mouth and in your heart, so that you can do it.

¹⁵ "See, I have set before you today life and good, death and evil. ¹⁶ If you obey the commandments of the Lord your God[a] that I command you today, by loving the Lord your God, by walking in his ways, and by keeping his commandments and his statutes and his rules,[b] then you shall live and multiply, and the Lord your God will bless you in the land that you are entering to take possession of it. ¹⁷ But if your heart turns away, and you will not hear, but are drawn away to worship other gods and serve them, ¹⁸ I declare to you today, that you shall surely perish. You shall not live long in the land that you are going over the Jordan to enter and possess. ¹⁹ I call heaven and earth to witness against you today, that I have set before you life and death, blessing and curse. Therefore choose life, that you and your offspring may live, ²⁰ loving the Lord your God, obeying his voice and holding fast to him, for he is your life and length of days, that you may dwell in the land that the Lord swore to your fathers, to Abraham, to Isaac, and to Jacob, to give them."

LESSON 4:
OUR RESPONSIBILITIES IN THIS AGREEMENT

_____
_____
_____
_____
_____

First, it is critical that we hear the instruction, understand it, and then follow it. Remember, this is always the process. It starts by asking what God has to say, how He clarifies it for us, and how we are to be obedient to what He says.

Word Meanings:

Hear/Listen: listen to, obey, to hear (*perceive by ear*), to hear of or concerning, hear (*have power to hear*), to hear with attention or interest, to understand

Set: to put, set, put on, put upon, appoint, assign, designate

Blessing: same word as good: good constitution or nature, useful, salutary, pleasant, agreeable, joyful, happy, excellent, distinguished, upright, honorable

Evil: evil (*adjective*), bad, disagreeable, malignant, unpleasant, giving pain, unhappiness, misery, displeasing

Walk: come, depart, proceed

Cleave: to cling, cleave to, to stay with, to be joined together

---

Read through Matthew 25:14-30 and write out what we are called to do as servants of the Master. What does that mean? How are we to carry this out, and what is the key to the process in carrying this out?

The Parable of the Talents
14 "For it will be like a man going on a journey, who called his servants[a] and entrusted to them his property. 15 To one he gave five talents,[b] to another two, to another one, to each according to his ability. Then he went away. 16 He who had received the five talents went at once and traded with them, and he made five talents more. 17 So also he who had the two talents made two talents more. 18 But he who had received the one talent went and dug in the ground and hid his master's money. 19 Now after a long time the master of those servants came and settled accounts with them. 20 And he who had received the five talents came forward, bringing five talents more, saying, 'Master, you delivered to me

LESSON 4:
OUR RESPONSIBILITIES IN THIS AGREEMENT

> five talents; here, I have made five talents more.' ²¹ His master said to him, 'Well done, good and faithful servant.[c] You have been faithful over a little; I will set you over much. Enter into the joy of your master.' ²² And he also who had the two talents came forward, saying, 'Master, you delivered to me two talents; here, I have made two talents more.' ²³ His master said to him, 'Well done, good and faithful servant. You have been faithful over a little; I will set you over much. Enter into the joy of your master.' ²⁴ He also who had received the one talent came forward, saying, 'Master, I knew you to be a hard man, reaping where you did not sow, and gathering where you scattered no seed, ²⁵ so I was afraid, and I went and hid your talent in the ground. Here, you have what is yours.' ²⁶ But his master answered him, 'You wicked and slothful servant! You knew that I reap where I have not sown and gather where I scattered no seed? ²⁷ Then you ought to have invested my money with the bankers, and at my coming I should have received what was my own with interest. ²⁸ So take the talent from him and give it to him who has the ten talents. ²⁹ For to everyone who has will more be given, and he will have an abundance. But from the one who has not, even what he has will be taken away.³⁰ And cast the worthless servant into the outer darkness. In that place there will be weeping and gnashing of teeth.'

_____
_____
_____
_____
_____

 Then, as we go through this parable, keep in mind the servants who were faithful (one with five talents or one with two) to the master's instructions. (Our Master sets the instructions, and our role is to be faithful. We are not to decide on our own what we are to do or what is a good idea but rather just follow His will for us and be obedient to that). We then are rewarded with bigger things (more authority, more responsibility) because we are faithful to small things. Never think bigger is better, as the important thing at this point is only to hear what He says. So, an instruction to disciple one person, or a child or grandchild, or spouse, etc. is as important as a big program; just follow His instruction, and He will bring great reward and joy through the covenant.

LESSON 4:
OUR RESPONSIBILITIES IN THIS AGREEMENT

Word Meanings:

Well Done: to be well off, fare well, prosper, acting well

Good: constitution or nature, useful, salutary, good, pleasant, agreeable, joyful, happy, excellent, distinguished, upright, honorable

Faithful: trusty, persons who show themselves faithful in the transaction of business, the execution of commands, or the discharge of official duties

Set: place, put, to set one over a thing (in charge of it), to appoint one to administer an office, to set down as, constitute, to declare, show to be; one who kept his plighted faith, worthy of trust, that can be relied on

Many: much, large

Enter: of entrance into any condition, state of things, society, employment

Joy: gladness, the joy received from you, the cause or occasion of joy

Do not get involved in civilian affairs.

Read through 2 Timothy 2:1-7 and write out the call to us as "soldiers of Christ." What are we to be careful of? What does that practically mean? What things in your life might you be entangled in that need to be adjusted or dropped?

A Good Soldier of Christ Jesus

2 You then, my child, be strengthened by the grace that is in Christ Jesus,[2] and what you have heard from me in the presence of many witnesses entrust to faithful men,[a] who will be able to teach others also. [3] Share in suffering as a good soldier of Christ Jesus. [4] No soldier gets entangled in civilian pursuits, since his aim is to please the one who enlisted him. [5] An athlete is not crowned unless he competes according to the rules. [6] It is the hard-working farmer who ought to have the first share of the crops. [7] Think over what I say, for the Lord will give you understanding in everything.

_____
_____
_____
_____
_____

LESSON 4:
OUR RESPONSIBILITIES IN THIS AGREEMENT

Civilian affairs are things that are outside of His work that He has given. We tend to get involved in too many things that bring distractions, burden, or heaviness. These things do not leave us with the ability to give our best to the work He has assigned to us as we have no margin, rest, peace, joy, etc. It is easy to get entangled because we decide on our own what things we want to do or get involved in but listening to His word is a critical piece of being obedient.

Word Meanings: **Entangle:** to inweave, of a thing: to entangle, involve in

Ponder the Path of Our Feet:

> **Read through Proverbs 4:26 and 5:21 and write out what is important to you as you walk forward in life. What exactly does this mean, and how would you fulfill this practically? Why is this so important?**
>
> ²⁶ Ponder[a] the path of your feet;
>   then all your ways will be sure.
>
> ²¹ For a man's ways are before the eyes of the Lord,
>   and he ponders[a] all his paths.

_____
_____
_____
_____

Our role is to consider and fully understand the path that God has set before us. This means that we are willing to spend the time to listen, process, and wait until we have clarity regarding our specific path.

Word Meanings: **Ponder:** to weigh, make level, balance, to weigh out, or make smooth
Way: road, distance, journey, manner, path, direction
Path: entrenchment, track, circumvallation
Goings: same as path: entrenchment, track, circumvallation

LESSON 4:
OUR RESPONSIBILITIES IN THIS AGREEMENT

> **Read through Isaiah 30:20-22 and write out how you process with God. What is He doing, and what do you do? Why is this so important versus just trying to figure things out on your own with your own sight and logic?**
>
> [20] And though the Lord give you the bread of adversity and the water of affliction, yet your Teacher will not hide himself anymore, but your eyes shall see your Teacher. [21] And your ears shall hear a word behind you, saying, "This is the way, walk in it," when you turn to the right or when you turn to the left. [22] Then you will defile your carved idols overlaid with silver and your gold-plated metal images. You will scatter them as unclean things. You will say to them, "Be gone!"

_____

_____

_____

_____

_____

These verses specifically say that we are to listen to the voice from behind. We are to do this so that we pay more attention to listening to the Holy Spirit, as opposed to relying on our own senses based upon what we see ahead of us (which is our normal approach). We are used to evaluating things based upon our own logic and only on the things we can understand in the natural. Because we need discernment and need to rely on what God knows is around the corner, in the future, we need to rely more on listening to His voice. Think of this analogy: When you walk someone who is blindfolded from the house to their car, they have to completely rely on your voice and not on anything that they can see since they cannot see. This is what we should be considering more as we ponder our paths.

Word Meanings: **Hear/Listen:** listen to, obey, to hear (*perceive by ear*), to hear of or concerning, hear (*have power to hear*), to hear with attention or interest, to understand

LESSON 4:
OUR RESPONSIBILITIES IN THIS AGREEMENT

> **Read through Psalm 86:11-12 and write out the important aspects of walking in God's path for us. How would you practically carry these out, and why are they so important to us?**
>
> [11] Teach me your way, O Lord,
>   that I may walk in your truth;
>   unite my heart to fear your name.
> [12] I give thanks to you, O Lord my God, with my whole heart,
>   and I will glorify your name forever.

_____
_____
_____
_____
_____

The three very important aspects of pondering and receiving understanding of God's paths for us are:

1. Being teachable—surrendered to His will, and not being prideful, stubborn, or deciding our own way.

2. Pursing truth—all the time. Determine what is the truth in every situation. Always be willing to receive new information—from any source—and let it impact what we understand about how He wants to show us His way. His way is always based upon truth.

3. Pray for and desire for Him to unite our hearts with His, to fear His name. This means we will always trust Him and believe what He has to say is true, even when it does not line up with our experience or desires or when the words are not fully understandable at the moment. Desire to know His will all the time above everything else.

LESSON 4:
OUR RESPONSIBILITIES IN THIS AGREEMENT

Word Meanings:
Unite: be joined, be united, firmness, faithfulness
Truth: sureness, reliability, stability, continuance, faithfulness, as spoken, of testimony and judgment, of divine instruction
Walk: come, depart, proceed
Teach: throw, shoot, cast
Way: road, distance, journey, manner, path, direction, habit, of course of life

LESSON 5:
OUR RESPONSIBILITIES IN THIS AGREEMENT (CON'T)

HOW DO WE WALK ALONG GOD'S COVENANT PATH FOR US? GAIN WISDOM/LISTEN/DELEGATE/BE TAUGHT.

As we now go deeper, we ask the question, "How do we receive God's will?" The answer is by receiving His wisdom through listening and being taught.

> **Read through Psalm 34:11-14 and write out the keys to receiving wisdom from God and desiring the covenant life of God. What does this look like to us in our life now? How would you apply this to your life today?**
>
> ¹¹ Come, O children, listen to me;
>   I will teach you the fear of the Lord.
> ¹² What man is there who desires life
>   and loves many days, that he may see good?
> ¹³ Keep your tongue from evil
>   and your lips from speaking deceit.
> ¹⁴ Turn away from evil and do good;
>   seek peace and pursue it.

> "As we learn to believe in the covenant, we must be faithful in what we pursue, accept, and stand on."

_____
_____
_____
_____
_____
_____

Draw the line between good and evil (what is not of God).

   In these verses we are to draw a line between good and evil. We are to make a fundamental decision that God's path is for us to pursue shalom (favor). We are to expect the best and go after the best. We are not to accept mediocrity (those things

LESSON 5:
OUR RESPONSIBILITIES IN THIS AGREEMENT (CON'T)

that are going to annoy, frustrate, irritate, bring misery, etc. in our lives). We must decide that we are not "to put up" with these things that are either mediocre or that continually annoy, frustrate, irritate, bring misery, etc. but to then pursue God's best: Shalom. Draw the line. We are not to speak it as we pursue the truth (discussed above), and we are not to be deceitful (withhold truth that might impact changing decisions that God has before us). As we learn to believe in the covenant, we must be faithful in what we pursue, accept, and stand on.

Word Meanings: **To Speak:** declare, converse, command, promise, warn, threaten, sing
Evil: evil (*adjective*), bad, disagreeable, malignant, unpleasant, giving pain, unhappiness, misery, displeasing
To Pursue Ardently: aim eagerly to secure
Peace/Shalom: completeness, soundness, welfare, completeness (*in number*), safety, soundness (*in body*), welfare, health, prosperity, quiet, tranquility, contentment, friendship, of human relationships, with God especially in covenant relationship
Seek: require, desire, exact, request, seek to find, to seek to secure
Good: constitution or nature, useful, salutary, pleasant, agreeable, joyful, happy, excellent, distinguished, upright, honorable
Depart: to turn aside, turn in, unto, depart from way, avoid

Read through Psalm 143:8-12 and write down how we are to pray to God to give us wisdom for our everyday life as we abide in His Word and seek His will.

[8] Let me hear in the morning of your steadfast love,
    for in you I trust.
Make me know the way I should go,
    for to you I lift up my soul.
[9] Deliver me from my enemies, O Lord!
    I have fled to you for refuge.[a]
[10] Teach me to do your will,
    for you are my God!
Let your good Spirit lead me
    on level ground!
[11] For your name's sake, O Lord, preserve my life!
    In your righteousness bring my soul out of trouble!

LESSON 5:
OUR RESPONSIBILITIES IN THIS AGREEMENT (CON'T)

> ¹² And in your steadfast love you will cut off my enemies,
> and you will destroy all the adversaries of my soul,
> for I am your servant.

_____
_____
_____
_____
_____

As we abide in the Word and receive wisdom for our paths, we should memorize this psalm and ask God to fulfill this for us all the time:

1. Cause us to hear His voice today.

2. Cause us to know the exact way we should walk (our path).

3. Deliver us from our enemies (may they not thwart His will because I walk away from the Kingdom and away from the covenant).

4. Teach me to do His will.

5. Lead me to the land of His promises – may He fulfill His promises as I follow Him.

6. Restore me fully as He promises.

Word Meanings:

Loving Kindness: covenant loyalty
Hear/Listen: listen to, obey, to hear (*perceive by ear*), to hear of or concerning, hear (*have power to hear*), to hear with attention or interest, to understand
To Know: learn to know, to perceive, to perceive and see, find out and discern, to discriminate, distinguish, to know by experience
Deliver: to ransom, redeem, rescue
To Teach: to be taught, be trained, exercise in
Lead: guide
Revive: to live, have life, remain alive, sustain life, live prosperously, live forever, be quickened, be alive, be restored to life or health

LESSON 5:
OUR RESPONSIBILITIES IN THIS AGREEMENT (CON'T)

Read through Exodus 18:17-27 and write out the truths about delegating. How are we to carry this out, and why is it so important in our life? In what practical ways can we fulfill this now in the things of our lives today?

17 Moses' father-in-law said to him, "What you are doing is not good. 18 You and the people with you will certainly wear yourselves out, for the thing is too heavy for you. You are not able to do it alone. 19 Now obey my voice; I will give you advice, and God be with you! You shall represent the people before God and bring their cases to God, 20 and you shall warn them about the statutes and the laws, and make them know the way in which they must walk and what they must do. 21 Moreover, look for able men from all the people, men who fear God, who are trustworthy and hate a bribe, and place such men over the people as chiefs of thousands, of hundreds, of fifties, and of tens. 22 And let them judge the people at all times. Every great matter they shall bring to you, but any small matter they shall decide themselves. So it will be easier for you, and they will bear the burden with you. 23 If you do this, God will direct you, you will be able to endure, and all this people also will go to their place in peace."

24 So Moses listened to the voice of his father-in-law and did all that he had said. 25 Moses chose able men out of all Israel and made them heads over the people, chiefs of thousands, of hundreds, of fifties, and of tens. 26 And they judged the people at all times. Any hard case they brought to Moses, but any small matter they decided themselves. 27 Then Moses let his father-in-law depart, and he went away to his own country.

_____
_____
_____
_____
_____

Part of the wisdom revealed by God is that we must learn to delegate. Walk through this discussion with Moses as he considers the advice of his father-in-law about the need to delegate. So many of us are doing too much and wearing

LESSON 5:
OUR RESPONSIBILITIES IN THIS AGREEMENT (CON'T)

ourselves out (which in the Hebrew is foolishness). Instead of doing too much, consider ways of delegating by hiring others to do things that can cost little but bring joy. Some are gifted at doing those things we need to offload to bring margin into our lives. These may be students, interns, maids, admins, lawn workers, etc. Then consider part timers. Be creative and be willing to part with some money to make life easier and more enjoyable by adding more margin to life. The question is simple: Are you wearing yourself out? Where can you delegate? Ask God to show you things you can offload without too much extra cost. Consider this both at a personal level and at a business level.

Word Meanings:

Wear Out: to be senseless, be foolish, to regard or treat as foolish, to treat with contempt, to sink or drop down, languish, wither and fall, fade
Teach: to admonish, warn, shine, send out light, be light, be shining
Show: same word as to know: learn to know, to perceive, to perceive and see, find out and discern, to discriminate, distinguish, to know by experience
Bear the Burden: to lift, bear up, carry, take

Wait on the Lord:

Waiting on the Lord is a big deal as we walk along the path and receive the promises of the covenant. We must remember that everything comes in His timing and not our own. This may be difficult as we wait or face what feels like a long delay. When promises are not fulfilled quickly (we always want the short term, or the immediate, and we expect things to happen instantly), we tend to take over and decide our own path. Waiting is critical to living in the covenant. He will deliver what He promises—but He is working all things according to His bigger story and His multiple dimensions. This is why He asks us to wait and not to take things in our own control and prevent what He is doing. The covenant life will happen. Trust and wait.

Read through Psalm 62:1-2, 62:5-8 and write out why it is so important to wait upon God showing us His way and His will in our lives. What does it mean to wait? What does He ask me to believe as I wait? Why?

My Soul Waits for God Alone
To the choirmaster: according to Jeduthun. A Psalm of David.
62 For God alone my soul waits in silence;
  from him comes my salvation.
² He alone is my rock and my salvation,
  my fortress; I shall not be greatly shaken.

LESSON 5:
OUR RESPONSIBILITIES IN THIS AGREEMENT (CON'T)

> ⁵ For God alone, O my soul, wait in silence,
>   for my hope is from him.
> ⁶ He only is my rock and my salvation,
>   my fortress; I shall not be shaken.
> ⁷ On God rests my salvation and my glory;
>   my mighty rock, my refuge is God.
> ⁸ Trust in him at all times, O people;
>   pour out your heart before him;
>   God is a refuge for us. *Selah*

_____
_____
_____
_____
_____

Our waiting is to occur at the soul level—the very essence of our being—a heart choice, and something settled in our soul silently (just God and me in process, not complaining, but dialoguing with Him as I continue to seek and understand His way for me): Why is that? Because:

1. He is my salvation and will provide the covenant, which is best and none better.

2. He is my defense and my security, which is the best place to stay.

3. I expect the best through the covenant (remember I have drawn this line above).

4. He is my rock and strength. I can fully trust that He will deliver the covenant, so I am willing and smart enough to wait for Him to deliver it.

Word Meanings: **Rock:** block of stone, boulder
Defense: high place, refuge, secure height, retreat
Not Be Moved: to be shaken, be moved, be overthrown, to dislodge, let fall, drop
Strength: might, material or physical

LESSON 5:
OUR RESPONSIBILITIES IN THIS AGREEMENT (CON'T)

> **Read through and write out what I can expect if I wait for God to act versus taking things in my own hands? Why is this going to be the better way to go? How can I live this out in my life now? Read Psalm 40:1-5.**
>
> My Help and My Deliverer
> To the choirmaster. A Psalm of David.
> **40** I waited patiently for the Lord;
>   he inclined to me and heard my cry.
> ² He drew me up from the pit of destruction,
>   out of the miry bog,
> and set my feet upon a rock,
>   making my steps secure.
> ³ He put a new song in my mouth,
>   a song of praise to our God.
> Many will see and fear,
>   and put their trust in the Lord.
> ⁴ Blessed is the man who makes
>   the Lord his trust,
> who does not turn to the proud,
>   to those who go astray after a lie!
> ⁵ You have multiplied, O Lord my God,
>   your wondrous deeds and your thoughts toward us;
>   none can compare with you!
> I will proclaim and tell of them,
>   yet they are more than can be told.

_____
_____
_____
_____
_____

    As I wait patiently (not take things back over in my own power or seek my own path), I will be lifted out of the pit, and He will establish my steps onto His covenant path. Why? Because I can trust that it will happen and do not need to be

LESSON 5:
OUR RESPONSIBILITIES IN THIS AGREEMENT (CON'T)

prideful by thinking I know better or by turning to lies by thinking there is a better way than God's way (which is still in process). Instead I will count on and experience His wonderful, supernatural works. Why then wouldn't I wait?

Word Meanings: **To Wait Patiently:** look for, hope, expect
Brought Me Up: to be taken up, be brought up, be taken away
Established: to be set up, be established, be fixed, to be firmly established
Steps: goings

Hope:

As we wait, it is particularly important that we live with hope, with the expectation for the covenant to be delivered to us—an expectation for good. Without it we will get discouraged, and God knows this, which is why He wants us to stay in hope throughout the process of waiting.

Read through Psalm 33:18-22 and write out how you would define hope, and why this is important in living out the life of the covenant. What specific areas of your life are you seeking hope?

18 Behold, the eye of the Lord is on those who fear him,
   on those who hope in his steadfast love,
19 that he may deliver their soul from death
   and keep them alive in famine.
20 Our soul waits for the Lord;
   he is our help and our shield.
21 For our heart is glad in him,
   because we trust in his holy name.
22 Let your steadfast love, O Lord, be upon us,
   even as we hope in you.

_____
_____
_____
_____
_____

LESSON 5:
OUR RESPONSIBILITIES IN THIS AGREEMENT (CON'T)

Our hope is in Him and His loyalty to the covenant. We can count on Him being our help and our protector and can fully trust that He will deliver the covenant to us. Our souls should rejoice continually because of this hope.

Covenant loyalty (mercy) is our hope.

> **Read through Romans 4:17-21 and note out how Abraham experienced hope. What did he trust, and what occurred in his life as a result? What was the role of hope in all this? Why is that important to us?**
>
> [17] as it is written, "I have made you the father of many nations"—in the presence of the God in whom he believed, who gives life to the dead and calls into existence the things that do not exist. [18] In hope he believed against hope, that he should become the father of many nations, as he had been told, "So shall your offspring be."[19] He did not weaken in faith when he considered his own body, which was as good as dead (since he was about a hundred years old), or when he considered the barrenness[a] of Sarah's womb. [20] No unbelief made him waver concerning the promise of God, but he grew strong in his faith as he gave glory to God, [21] fully convinced that God was able to do what he had promised.

_____
_____
_____
_____
_____
_____

This describes Abraham who should not have had any hope because he had passed the point at which he and Sarah were physically able to have children. Nevertheless, because of the promise that was given, he believed God who is able to bring things back to life and call those things that do not exist as if they were. No circumstance is beyond His ability to make happen, even though it appears there is little or no chance, because nothing is too difficult for Him. If God has spoken a promise, regardless of the current circumstances and what it appears we might need for the promise to be fulfilled, we are to continue to believe that it will

LESSON 5:
OUR RESPONSIBILITIES IN THIS AGREEMENT (CON'T)

be fulfilled. We are to maintain hope and be fully persuaded that what God has spoken will be performed: hope.

Word Meanings:

Hope: expectation of good
Believed: to think to be true, to be persuaded of, to credit, place confidence in
Faith: conviction of the truth of anything, belief; in the conviction or belief respecting man's relationship to God and divine things, generally with the included idea of trust and holy fervor born of faith and joined with it, of the thing believed, to credit, have confidence
Not Waver: to be at variance with one's self, hesitate, doubt
Assured: to make one certain
To Persuade: convince one, to be persuaded, fully convinced or assured

> **Read through Romans 15:13 and write out the elements of our prayer as we seek hope. What can we believe that God will provide, and what can we expect in our lives?**
>
> ¹³ May the God of hope fill you with all joy and peace in believing, so that by the power of the Holy Spirit you may abound in hope.

_____
_____
_____
_____
_____
_____

As we are struggling with our faith to stay in hope, we are to pray that God will fill us with joy and shalom to believe by the power of the Holy Spirit that we maintain our hope. It is His work, so we do not have to struggle on our own to receive hope but rather to ask through the power of the Spirit to give us hope.

LESSON 5:
OUR RESPONSIBILITIES IN THIS AGREEMENT (CON'T)

Word Meanings:

Joy: gladness, the joy received from you, the cause or occasion of joy

Peace/Shalom: peace between individuals, (i.e., harmony), concord, security, safety, prosperity, felicity, (because peace and harmony make and keep things safe and prosperous)

Believed: to think to be true, to be persuaded of, to credit, place confidence in, of the thing believed

Hope: in a religious sense, to wait for salvation with joy and full confidence

Power: strength power, ability, inherent power, power residing in a thing by virtue of its nature, or which a person or thing exerts and puts forth, power for performing miracles, moral power and excellence of soul, the power and influence which belong to riches and wealth

Trust:

Waiting in hope fully depends on trust. Do I believe God, what He speaks, and that He will deliver the covenant life as promised?

Read through Proverbs 3:1-15 and write out all the truths about what we are to do to build trust in God; and what God promises as we build trust in God. Trust in the Lord with All Your Heart

3 My son, do not forget my teaching,
  but let your heart keep my commandments,
2 for length of days and years of life
  and peace they will add to you.
3 Let not steadfast love and faithfulness forsake you;
  bind them around your neck;
  write them on the tablet of your heart.
4 So you will find favor and good success[a]
  in the sight of God and man.
5 Trust in the Lord with all your heart,
  and do not lean on your own understanding.
6 In all your ways acknowledge him,
  and he will make straight your paths.
7 Be not wise in your own eyes;
  fear the Lord, and turn away from evil.
8 It will be healing to your flesh[b]
  and refreshment[c] to your bones.
9 Honor the Lord with your wealth
  and with the firstfruits of all your produce;

LESSON 5:
OUR RESPONSIBILITIES IN THIS AGREEMENT (CON'T)

> ¹⁰ then your barns will be filled with plenty,
>   and your vats will be bursting with wine.
> ¹¹ My son, do not despise the Lord's discipline
>   or be weary of his reproof,
> ¹² for the Lord reproves him whom he loves,
>   as a father the son in whom he delights.
>
> Blessed Is the One Who Finds Wisdom
> ¹³ Blessed is the one who finds wisdom,
>   and the one who gets understanding,
> ¹⁴ for the gain from her is better than gain from silver
>   and her profit better than gold.
> ¹⁵ She is more precious than jewels,
>   and nothing you desire can compare with her.

_____
_____
_____
_____
_____

All of the verses in Proverbs 3 helps us understand the ingredients to building trust:

1. Keep His instructions

2. Remember covenant loyalty and truth as the essence of our relationship with God (keep these front and center)

3. Trust in God first and foremost with the essence of our soul. Get this settled; and do not lean on our own understanding (do not rely on our natural way of making decisions but listen and follow His will)

4. Follow Him in all our ways and let Him direct each step (not some steps, but all steps)

LESSON 5:
OUR RESPONSIBILITIES IN THIS AGREEMENT (CON'T)

5. Do not be wise in our own eyes by thinking we know better (we never do)

6. Fear the Lord (know that He knows more than we do, and His ways are best and none better, so seek Him always)

7. Depart from evil. Do not accept mediocrity or believe that things that irritate, annoy, or frustrate are to be a normal way of life (they are not)

8. Always tithe, as this is a test of our heart and attached to a key promise of the covenant (abundance)

9. Be willing to be corrected whenever we stray because we incorrectly went our own way

10. Always pursue wisdom and understanding as these will lead us to the best: the covenant life!

Word Meanings:

Trust: to have confidence, be confident, to be bold, to be secure
To Lean On: trust in, support
Own Understanding: discernment
Direct: to make right, make smooth, make straight, to lead, direct, lead straight along
Wise: wise (*man*); skillful (*in technical work*); wise (*in administration*), shrewd, crafty, cunning, wily, subtle, learned, shrewd (*class of men*), prudent

---

Read through Psalm 20:7-8 and write down the choice we have in whom we can trust. As we trust in God, what will be the result? Why is this so important to us?

⁷ Some trust in chariots and some in horses,
  but we trust in the name of the Lord our God.
⁸ They collapse and fall,
  but we rise and stand upright.

LESSON 5:
OUR RESPONSIBILITIES IN THIS AGREEMENT (CON'T)

_____
_____
_____
_____
_____

And thus, do not trust in your own strength or things that you think can provide you success. Work at it by trusting only in God and what He says. He knows! Do not come with your own answers or your own great ideas – just trust Him!

Word Meanings: **Trust:** to have confidence, be confident, to be bold, to be secure
Name: reputation, fame, glory, the Name (*as designation of God*), memorial, monument

LESSON 6:
OUR RESPONSIBILITIES IN THIS AGREEMENT (CON'T)

STAY IN, OFFER PEACE.

As we have learned, a key aspect of receiving the covenant is to be living in the Kingdom; and living in the Kingdom means we are living in peace (shalom). Since our lives involve other people, those who are not living in the Kingdom, this can be quite the challenge. One of the big strategies (schemes) of the enemy is to use self-centered, ungodly people to draw us out of the Kingdom to steal our peace and captivate us through our anger, envy, unforgiveness, jealousy, etc. Here, we are going to go into a deep discussion of this important understanding of how to stay in the Kingdom where we can offer peace to others so that we remain in the Kingdom and receive the benefits of the covenant.

"Peace only comes from Him, as our mind and soul are stayed (kept) on Him."

Read through Isaiah 26:2-5 and 26:12 and write out the role of peace and how we stay in peace. How do we live this out right now in the issues of our life?

² Open the gates,
 that the righteous nation that keeps faith may enter in.
³ You keep him in perfect peace
 whose mind is stayed on you,
 because he trusts in you.
⁴ Trust in the Lord forever,
 for the Lord God is an everlasting rock.
⁵ For he has humbled
 the inhabitants of the height,
 the lofty city.
He lays it low, lays it low to the ground,
 casts it to the dust.

¹² O Lord, you will ordain peace for us,
 for you have indeed done for us all our works.

LESSON 6:
OUR RESPONSIBILITIES IN THIS AGREEMENT (CON'T)

_____
_____
_____
_____
_____

Peace only comes from Him, as our mind and soul are stayed (kept) on Him. We are called to trust in, abide in, stay with, and remain in Him as He gives us His peace (which is perfect, complete). He does this work in us. The key is that we cannot work at this ourselves. When we lack peace (because we are troubled, worried, anxious, frustrated, angry, etc.), we cannot fix it by trying to get back to peace on our own. Why? Because it is His work, and the only way to obtain it is to receive it by repenting and going back to the abiding relationship and having Him restore His peace to us.

Word Meanings:

Keep: to guard, watch, watch over, to preserve, guard from dangers, observe, guard with fidelity, keep secret
Mind: purpose, imagination, device (*intellectual framework*)
Stayed: to lean, lay, rest, support, put, uphold, lean upon
Perfect Peace: shalom
To Ordain: establish

Read through Isaiah 53:3-6 and write out on what basis can we receive and live in peace. Is there anything we can do to earn it? What then is the key to staying in peace?

3 He was despised and rejected[a] by men,
    a man of sorrows[b] and acquainted with[c] grief;[d]
and as one from whom men hide their faces[e]
    he was despised, and we esteemed him not.
4 Surely he has borne our griefs
    and carried our sorrows;
yet we esteemed him stricken,
    smitten by God, and afflicted.
5 But he was pierced for our transgressions;
    he was crushed for our iniquities;

LESSON 6:
OUR RESPONSIBILITIES IN THIS AGREEMENT (CON'T)

> upon him was the chastisement that brought us peace,
>   and with his wounds we are healed.
> ⁶ All we like sheep have gone astray;
>   we have turned—every one—to his own way;
> and the Lord has laid on him
>   the iniquity of us all.

_____
_____
_____
_____
_____
_____

    How is this possible? This verse (and the next) answers this question. First, He is our peace because He took on the penalty for God's wrath against sin, was wounded for our iniquity, transgression, and sickness, and became our peace. He can now offer us this peace through our belief as we receive these gifts directly from Him, not by anything we do to earn it (we cannot). There is no other way to live in the covenant life.

Word Meanings:

Borne: bear, carry, support, sustain, endure, to take, take away, carry off, forgive
Grief: sickness
Stricken: be defeated
Iniquities: perversity, depravity, iniquity, guilt or punishment of iniquity
To Wound: (*fatally*), bore through, pierce, bore
Transgression: rebellion
To Heal: make healthful, of God, healer, physician (*of men*), of hurts of nations involving restored favor (*figuratively*)

LESSON 6:
OUR RESPONSIBILITIES IN THIS AGREEMENT (CON'T)

> **Read through Colossians 1:15-23 and write out the position of Christ regarding our world and our circumstances. Then note what you see is His heart toward our life circumstances. What can we then expect and receive? Why?**
>
> The Preeminence of Christ
> 15 He is the image of the invisible God, the firstborn of all creation. 16 For by[f] him all things were created, in heaven and on earth, visible and invisible, whether thrones or dominions or rulers or authorities—all things were created through him and for him. 17 And he is before all things, and in him all things hold together. 18 And he is the head of the body, the church. He is the beginning, the firstborn from the dead, that in everything he might be preeminent. 19 For in him all the fullness of God was pleased to dwell, 20 and through him to reconcile to himself all things, whether on earth or in heaven, making peace by the blood of his cross.
>
> 21 And you, who once were alienated and hostile in mind, doing evil deeds, 22 he has now reconciled in his body of flesh by his death, in order to present you holy and blameless and above reproach before him, 23 if indeed you continue in the faith, stable and steadfast, not shifting from the hope of the gospel that you heard, which has been proclaimed in all creation[g] under heaven, and of which I, Paul, became a minister.

_____
_____
_____
_____
_____
_____

    And, having made this peace, which is now available to all of us who believe, He has reconciled all things back to Himself. He is now restoring the life of peace (shalom) to us through the covenant, not by us earning it or doing something to get it, but only by abiding, and putting Him preeminent—first in everything. Go to Him first, always, and just receive it. When we do, He will put us in perfect peace

LESSON 6:
OUR RESPONSIBILITIES IN THIS AGREEMENT (CON'T)

(remember, this is the only way to receive it). Unless we learn this profound truth, we will continue living without peace; and the harder we try to get that peace ourselves, the more we will live without it.

Word Meanings: **To Reconcile Completely:** to reconcile back again, bring back a former state of harmony
All Things: individually, each, every, any, all, the whole, everyone, all things, everything
To Make Peace (shalom): establish harmony

> **Read through Philippians 4:6-7 and write out the keys to receiving and staying in peace. As you consider your life situations right now, put these to practice and write out what is going to bring you peace.**
>
> ⁶ do not be anxious about anything, but in everything by prayer and supplication with thanksgiving let your requests be made known to God. ⁷ And the peace of God, which surpasses all understanding, will guard your hearts and your minds in Christ Jesus.

_____
_____
_____
_____
_____

So, with this understanding, we then are to be anxious for nothing, but in everything gives thanks (wait, be in hope, expect the covenant life to be delivered no matter what, and know that we are in process already today), and then dialogue with God to hear what He has to say about all our issues of life so we receive His wisdom, and we will receive His peace (which passes all understanding, since it is not ours but His). Remember, this is not our work but His.

Word Meanings: **Request:** petition
To Make Known: to become known, be recognized, to know, to gain knowledge of, have thorough knowledge of

LESSON 6:
OUR RESPONSIBILITIES IN THIS AGREEMENT (CON'T)

Peace: shalom
Surpassing: to stand out, rise above, overtop, to be above, be superior in rank, authority, power, the prominent men, rulers, to excel, to be superior, better than, to surpass

So, how do we handle those who are coming against us, oppose us, not willing to resolve conflict with us, particularly other Christians or relatives? This is a major discussion since much of the Christian church has not taught about this. Often, we have heard that we are just to put up with it and allow people to hurt us. But this, which is not truth, only breeds real anger, un-forgiveness, and frustration. These, then, bring people into guilt and discouragement. Let's walk through this in detail:

> **Read through Romans 12:9-20 and write out the keys to handling conflict with those who oppose you. How would you interpret what it means to bless those who curse you? Would you hope for God's wrath? Or have the feeling that "vengeance is mine, sayeth the Lord?" These all go together and are important in how we handle those who are against us, hurting us, opposing us. How would you remain in peace (in your heart level, not through some task) in the middle of all this?**
>
> Marks of the True Christian
> [9] Let love be genuine. Abhor what is evil; hold fast to what is good. [10] Love one another with brotherly affection. Outdo one another in showing honor. [11] Do not be slothful in zeal, be fervent in spirit,[a] serve the Lord. [12] Rejoice in hope, be patient in tribulation, be constant in prayer. [13] Contribute to the needs of the saints and seek to show hospitality.
>
> [14] Bless those who persecute you; bless and do not curse them. [15] Rejoice with those who rejoice, weep with those who weep. [16] Live in harmony with one another. Do not be haughty, but associate with the lowly.[b] Never be wise in your own sight. [17] Repay no one evil for evil, but give thought to do what is honorable in the sight of all. [18] If possible, so far as it depends on you, live peaceably with all. [19] Beloved, never avenge yourselves, but leave it[c] to the wrath of God, for it is written, "Vengeance is mine, I will repay, says the Lord." [20] To the contrary, "if your enemy is hungry, feed him; if he is thirsty, give him something to drink; for by so doing you will heap burning coals on his head."

LESSON 6:
OUR RESPONSIBILITIES IN THIS AGREEMENT (CON'T)

_____
_____
_____
_____
_____

Here are the key points:

1. Do not be a hypocrite. Stay true to your heart and stay in truth through this all.

2. Stay where we already know. Draw a line between good and evil, expect the covenant life, and do not accept mediocrity or expect a life of frustration, annoyance, irritation, or hardship. These need not be normal (this includes hard relationships).

3. Be kind and loving toward others. Always do and speak to others with honor and respect.

4. Be in prayer (in relationship with God and get your marching orders from Him).

5. Be hospitable. Have a desire to be friendly and enjoy being around others.

6. Consider these verses regarding those who persecute (oppose, come against, want to hurt you):

    a. Verse 18. As much as possible live peaceably with them. In other words, do not do anything that would give them cause to be against you because you were not honorable, treated them poorly, took action against them, etc.

    b. Do not take revenge yourself. It is not your role or right to do so (which will only consume you and draw you into the Satan's battle ground, ultimately resulting in being drawn away from the Kingdom and into the flesh).

    c. Give place to God's wrath for He will take vengeance. You can count on it. Why? This is part of the promise of the covenant. He will bless those who bless you and curse those who curse you. He will bring His wrath for sure. What does it mean when we say they are cursing you? There is an unwillingness to sit down with you and discuss truth and work toward reconciliation; which goes back to the above definitions of you being kind and loving, respectful, and peaceable. You must always be willing to go

LESSON 6:
OUR RESPONSIBILITIES IN THIS AGREEMENT (CON'T)

to truth and work toward reconciliation, which is the way of pursuing blessing. You do not have to agree, just be willing to pursue God's will together until you see God's answer (His will, which is best and none better). Unwillingness to do so is why there is cursing. A person has decided in the flesh that they are not willing to be respectful with you and pursue truth together with you and thus are going to receive the curse of God. Your action at that point is to get out of the way and let God fulfill His wrath or purpose. You, then, are not to rescue, keep trying to make things work, take revenge yourself, etc. Get out of the way and know that God will handle things for His purpose.

How does this mesh then with verse 14 (bless those who persecute you—bless and do not curse)? We already have seen that it is not our place to curse—it is God's. So, how are we to bless since we are to get out of the way and let God curse? What is the remedy for any of us to be released from God's curses? Repentance. We are to bless them by praying that they would repent, which is their only remedy. We have to pray that they understand what they are called to do, or that someone will show them, and that they will repent. This is the only way of being blessed as that is the only way to stop the curse, and it will. And if they do, we are to rejoice, welcome them back, and re-engage if they now have a heart to discuss truth and work through this to reconcile with us.

Word Meanings:

Abhor: dislike, have a horror of
Cleave: to join or fasten firmly together, to join one's self to
Good: pleasant, agreeable (to the senses); pleasant (to the higher nature), excellent, rich, valuable in estimation: glad, happy, prosperous
Affection: prone to love, loving tenderly
Bless: to consecrate a thing with solemn prayers
Persecute: in any way whatever to harass, trouble, molest one; to be mistreated, suffer persecution on account of something; curse, doom, imprecate evil upon
Recompense: to deliver, to give away for one's own profit what is one's own, to sell; to pay off, discharge what is due
Honest: beautiful, handsome, excellent, eminent, choice, surpassing, precious, useful, suitable, commendable, admirable
Avenge: a thing to punish a person for a thing
Vengeance: a revenging, punishment; meeting out of justice; doing justice to all parties; the word also has the sense of acquittal and carries the sense of vindication
Repay: in a bad sense, penalty and vengeance

LESSON 6:
OUR RESPONSIBILITIES IN THIS AGREEMENT (CON'T)

> **Read through 2 Timothy 2:20-26 and write out what God asks us to do with people who have not only come against us but who are not willing to work things out with us and are continuing to hurt and oppose us? Why is this important to our heart and maintaining our positive life with God?**
>
> [20] Now in a great house there are not only vessels of gold and silver but also of wood and clay, some for honorable use, some for dishonorable. [21] Therefore, if anyone cleanses himself from what is dishonorable,[a] he will be a vessel for honorable use, set apart as holy, useful to the master of the house, ready for every good work. [22] So flee youthful passions and pursue righteousness, faith, love, and peace, along with those who call on the Lord from a pure heart. [23] Have nothing to do with foolish, ignorant controversies; you know that they breed quarrels. [24] And the Lord's servant[b] must not be quarrelsome but kind to everyone, able to teach, patiently enduring evil, [25] correcting his opponents with gentleness. God may perhaps grant them repentance leading to a knowledge of the truth, [26] and they may come to their senses and escape from the snare of the devil, after being captured by him to do his will.

_____
_____
_____
_____
_____

    We are to pray that they may come to their senses to repent and be released from being taken captive to the will of Satan, that they get back their own will so that they can repent. We are not to argue, debate, or get involved in foolish disputes—it does absolutely no good. It is far better to teach gently if they are willing to receive, and also to intercede with prayer that they would repent. This is how we bless those who are opposing and persecuting us.

Word Meanings:

Able to Teach: apt and skillful in teaching
Forbearing: patience
Gentleness: mildness of disposition, gentleness of spirit, meekness
Come to Their Senses: to return to soberness
Taken Captive: to take alive, to take, catch, capture

LESSON 6:
OUR RESPONSIBILITIES IN THIS AGREEMENT (CON'T)

Read through Luke 10:1-13 and write out how we are to work things out with people with whom we have conflicts and who oppose us. Why is this important to our heart and maintaining our freedom and our life with God?

Jesus Sends Out the Seventy-Two

10 After this the Lord appointed seventy-two[a] others and sent them on ahead of him, two by two, into every town and place where he himself was about to go. ² And he said to them, "The harvest is plentiful, but the laborers are few. Therefore pray earnestly to the Lord of the harvest to send out laborers into his harvest. ³ Go your way; behold, I am sending you out as lambs in the midst of wolves. ⁴ Carry no moneybag, no knapsack, no sandals, and greet no one on the road. ⁵ Whatever house you enter, first say, 'Peace be to this house!' ⁶ And if a son of peace is there, your peace will rest upon him. But if not, it will return to you. ⁷ And remain in the same house, eating and drinking what they provide, for the laborer deserves his wages. Do not go from house to house. ⁸ Whenever you enter a town and they receive you, eat what is set before you. ⁹ Heal the sick in it and say to them, 'The kingdom of God has come near to you.' ¹⁰ But whenever you enter a town and they do not receive you, go into its streets and say, ¹¹ 'Even the dust of your town that clings to our feet we wipe off against you. Nevertheless know this, that the kingdom of God has come near.' ¹² I tell you, it will be more bearable on that day for Sodom than for that town.

Woe to Unrepentant Cities

¹³ "Woe to you, Chorazin! Woe to you, Bethsaida! For if the mighty works done in you had been done in Tyre and Sidon, they would have repented long ago, sitting in sackcloth and ashes.

_____
_____
_____
_____
_____

LESSON 6:
OUR RESPONSIBILITIES IN THIS AGREEMENT (CON'T)

The following gives us the prescription for how and where we are to spend our time—and it involves our peace. First, in order for us to offer our peace, we must be in peace (shalom) ourselves. We cannot give away what we do not have. Then, we offer our peace to others. We invite them to get into the Word, to learn what it means to abide and learn to live the covenant life. It matters not the current state of life they are in (perhaps they are in great difficulty, doing awful things, etc. but we must recognize that it is not our place to judge anything about them, only to offer our peace. We need to hope they have a willingness to accept the offer. If they say yes (I am willing to get into the Word and learn this), then we are to stay with them and help them learn this. We are not to have a program but to walk with them as God so leads. Remember, we are sheep dogs being led by the Holy Spirit and giving it away as He so instructs.

Also, realize that we are not therapists, so our role is not to give them our advice regarding how to live or to try to "fix" them. Instead, we are simply to teach them how to abide and how to live the covenant life. This is God's work through His Word and not ours. They have to agree to get in the Word, and then actually do it based on the assignments you give them. This will be a true indicator of receiving your peace. If they don't do both (agree and do), then they have rejected your peace. If they have rejected your peace, you are not to take it personally (they are not rejecting you but God) but are to take back your peace (do not leave any of your shalom with them) and then dust off your feet (do not allow any of their issues or rejection stick to you). You need to release this rejection or sadness that they will not receive what you know will give them the beautiful covenant life and move on. Do not waste your time, and do not stay in sadness. Instead, remain in joy; do not take on the burden. If it is someone whom you do not have any relationship with, you can literally forget it; if it is someone you know or are going to spend time with (like a relative), dusting your feet off is not ignoring but rather not taking on the emotional burden of their choices. You can then pray that some day they will have a desire again to receive your peace. If they ever do, because you live in forgiveness, you will happily offer it again.

Word Meanings:

Worthy: weighing, having weight, having the weight of another thing of like value, worth as much, befitting, congruous, corresponding to a thing

Peace: shalom

Rest: to cause to rest upon anything: to rest upon anything, to settle upon, fix its abode upon

Return: to turn back

Abide: remain, reference to place, to sojourn, tarry, not to depart, continue to be present, to be held, kept, continually

LESSON 6:
OUR RESPONSIBILITIES IN THIS AGREEMENT (CON'T)

Not Receive: not to take with the hand, to take hold of, take up, of the thing offered in speaking, teaching, instructing, to receive favorably, give ear to, embrace, make one's own, approve;

Rejects: to do away with, to set aside, disregard, to thwart the efficacy of anything, nullify, make void

Find out who is worthy.

> **As we continue to have a desire to stay in process with people who are in conflict with us or who oppose us, we are to determine who is worthy to continue that process. Read through Colossians 1:9-12 and write out how we determine who is worthy and thus would give us the encouragement to stay in process.**
>
> [9] And so, from the day we heard, we have not ceased to pray for you, asking that you may be filled with the knowledge of his will in all spiritual wisdom and understanding, [10] so as to walk in a manner worthy of the Lord, fully pleasing to him: bearing fruit in every good work and increasing in the knowledge of God; [11] being strengthened with all power, according to his glorious might, for all endurance and patience with joy; [12] giving thanks[d] to the Father, who has qualified you[e] to share in the inheritance of the saints in light.

_____
_____
_____
_____
_____

Who is worthy? It is really simple: those who have a desire to know God and be filled with the knowledge of His will. They should have the desire to abide with Him, follow Him, and live in the covenant life.

LESSON 6:
OUR RESPONSIBILITIES IN THIS AGREEMENT (CON'T)

Word Meanings:

Filled: make full, to fill up, i.e. to fill to the full, to cause to abound, to furnish or supply liberally, I abound, I am liberally supplied, to render full, i.e. to complete, to fill to the top: so that nothing shall be wanting, to full measure, fill to the brim

Wisdom: broad and full of intelligence; used of the knowledge of very diverse matters, the wisdom, which belongs to men, specifically the varied knowledge of things human and divine, acquired by acuteness and experience, and summed up in maxims and proverbs, the science and learning, the act of interpreting dreams and always giving the sagest advice, the intelligence evinced in discovering the meaning of some mysterious number or vision skill in the management of affairs, devout and proper prudence in intercourse with men not disciples of Christ, skill and discretion in imparting Christian truth, the knowledge and practice of the requisites for godly and upright living

Understanding: perception with the thing perceived

Fruitful: bear fruit

Good: constitution or nature, useful, salutary, pleasant, agreeable, joyful, happy, excellent, distinguished, upright, honorable

Work: business, employment, that which any one is occupied, that which one undertakes to do, enterprise, undertaking, any product whatever, any thing accomplished by hand, art, industry, or mind

Might: power, dunamis

Longsuffering: patience, endurance, perseverance

Joy: gladness

Partaker: apart as distinct from the whole, an assigned part, a portion, share

Inheritance: an object used in casting or drawing lots, which was either a pebble, or a potsherd, or a bit of wood, the lots of several persons concerned, inscribed with their names, were thrown together into a vase, which was then shaken, and he whose lot fell out first upon the ground was the one chosen, what is obtained by lot, allotted portion

---

Read through Colossians 3:15 and write out how we use peace to determine our decisions and whether we are walking with God in His Kingdom or in self and not following Him? How does this work practically for us?

¹⁵ And let the peace of Christ rule in your hearts, to which indeed you were called in one body. And be thankful.

LESSON 6:
OUR RESPONSIBILITIES IN THIS AGREEMENT (CON'T)

_____
_____
_____
_____
_____

We are to live all of our life letting peace (shalom) umpire our life. An umpire calls things clearly (fair/foul; ball/strike; safe/out), so we know whether we are at peace or not. If we are, then we are living in the abiding relationship, in the Kingdom, in the covenant. If not in peace, then something has gone wrong as we are in the flesh. The remedy, then, is repentance. Do not try to fix something on your own. Realize instead that we are in the flesh, that we need to repent, and then return to the abiding relationship where He will lead and guide us as we surrender to the King in the Kingdom. Do not confuse repentance with confession. Many people make this mistake and keep traveling along the path of self-forgetting to return to the abiding relationship. This relationship is critical to living in the Kingdom and the covenant life. This is why it is so important to let peace umpire.

Word Meanings: **Peace Between Individuals:** harmony, concord
Security: safety, prosperity, felicity, (because peace and harmony make and keep things safe and prosperous)
Rule: umpire
A Word: uttered by a living voice, embodies a concept or idea, what someone has said

LESSON 7:
OUR RESPONSIBILITIES IN THIS AGREEMENT (CON'T)

UNITY.

> **Read through Psalm 133 and write out the benefit of dwelling and living in unity. What happens there? Why? Who is unity with? What does this mean for our lives?**
>
> When Brothers Dwell in Unity
> A Song of Ascents. Of David.
> **133** Behold, how good and pleasant it is
>   when brothers dwell in unity![a]
> ² It is like the precious oil on the head,
>   running down on the beard,
> on the beard of Aaron,
>   running down on the collar of his robes!
> ³ It is like the dew of Hermon,
>   which falls on the mountains of Zion!
> For there the Lord has commanded the blessing,
>   life forevermore.

> "We thus need to be careful what we are sowing—since we are always sowing something."

_____
_____
_____
_____
_____

    As we are to continue our life in the covenant, which requires us to stay in the Kingdom and stay on His path, in His will, we are to remain in unity with our spouse, with another close spirit-led friend who is walking in the covenant. Why? Because there, we discover God's will as He confirms it through unity (and remember unity is not an agreement between two people but between two people and the Holy Spirit, which is spiritual and is confirmed in the Spirit and is the very definition of unity). "There" (when you reach unity) God COMMANDS BLESSING! Why, then, would you not always and every time go to unity? And what is the blessing? It is the covenant—blessed to be a blessing.

LESSON 7:
OUR RESPONSIBILITIES IN THIS AGREEMENT (CON'T)

Word Meanings:
Good: constitution or nature, useful, salutary, pleasant, agreeable, joyful, happy, excellent, distinguished, upright, honorable
Pleasant: delightful, sweet, lovely, agreeable
Dwell: remain in
Unity: union, unitedness, agreement, oneness
Commanded: ordered
Blessing: gifts, prosperity

Sowing/Reaping:

Another interesting principle of the covenant life is that we are to be sowing certain things (a very active process) that contribute to the reaping and are part and parcel to receiving the blessing. We thus need to be careful what we are sowing—since we are always sowing something.

Read through Genesis 26:12-14 and write out the basic principle of sowing and reaping. Why is that important for us to understand in our lives?

¹² And Isaac sowed in that land and reaped in the same year a hundredfold. The Lord blessed him, ¹³ and the man became rich, and gained more and more until he became very wealthy. ¹⁴ He had possessions of flocks and herds and many servants, so that the Philistines envied him.

_____
_____
_____
_____
_____

Remember this simple principle: sowing results in reaping: a hundredfold and is a blessing from God; and it continued (each year he sowed more and reaped more) and became very prosperous!

Word Meanings:
To Sow: scatter seed, producing, yielding seed, to be sown, to become pregnant, be made pregnant
Gained More Wealth: to grow, become great or important, promote, make powerful, praise, magnify, do great things, to grow up, to be magnified
Became Rich: to grow, become great or important, promote, make powerful, praise, magnify, do great things

LESSON 7:
OUR RESPONSIBILITIES IN THIS AGREEMENT (CON'T)

> **Read through Psalm 97:11-12 and write out the various things we are to sow (define what these mean) and the benefits we are to reap. What will these mean to us in our lives?**
>
> [11] Light is sown[a] for the righteous,
>   and joy for the upright in heart.
> [12] Rejoice in the Lord, O you righteous,
>   and give thanks to his holy name!

_____
_____
_____
_____
_____

Sow light to reap gladness, pleasure, and happiness. The key is to stay in the light, to stay on His path, following His steps, which will be light. This is why unity is so important because it helps us stay in His light.

Word Meanings: **Gladness:** joy, mirth, gaiety, pleasure, joy (of God), glad result, happy issue
Light: of life, light of prosperity, light of instruction
To Sow: scatter seed, producing, yielding seed, to be sown, to become pregnant, be made pregnant, to produce seed

> **One thing we are universally called to sow is a tithe of our income. We are to trust God and do so generously and out of our heart. If we sow generously, we will reap generously, but if we sow sparingly, we will reap sparingly. The Lord shows us the truth of all this further with 1 Chronicles 29 and Malachi 3.**
>
> Offerings for the Temple
> **29** And David the king said to all the assembly, "Solomon my son, whom alone God has chosen, is young and inexperienced, and the work is great, for the palace will not be for man but for the Lord God. ² So I have provided for the house of my God, so far as I was able, the gold for the things of gold, the silver for the things of silver, and the bronze for the things of bronze, the iron for the things of iron, and wood

LESSON 7:
OUR RESPONSIBILITIES IN THIS AGREEMENT (CON'T)

for the things of wood, besides great quantities of onyx and stones for setting, antimony, colored stones, all sorts of precious stones and marble. 3 Moreover, in addition to all that I have provided for the holy house, I have a treasure of my own of gold and silver, and because of my devotion to the house of my God I give it to the house of my God: 4 3,000 talents[a] of gold, of the gold of Ophir, and 7,000 talents of refined silver, for overlaying the walls of the house,[b] 5 and for all the work to be done by craftsmen, gold for the things of gold and silver for the things of silver. Who then will offer willingly, consecrating himself[c] today to the Lord?" 6 Then the leaders of fathers' houses made their freewill offerings, as did also the leaders of the tribes, the commanders of thousands and of hundreds, and the officers over the king's work. 7 They gave for the service of the house of God 5,000 talents and 10,000 darics[d] of gold, 10,000 talents of silver, 18,000 talents of bronze and 100,000 talents of iron. 8 And whoever had precious stones gave them to the treasury of the house of the Lord, in the care of Jehiel the Gershonite. 9 Then the people rejoiced because they had given willingly, for with a whole heart they had offered freely to the Lord. David the king also rejoiced greatly.

David Prays in the Assembly
10 Therefore David blessed the Lord in the presence of all the assembly. And David said: "Blessed are you, O Lord, the God of Israel our father, forever and ever. 11 Yours, O Lord, is the greatness and the power and the glory and the victory and the majesty, for all that is in the heavens and in the earth is yours. Yours is the kingdom, O Lord, and you are exalted as head above all. 12 Both riches and honor come from you, and you rule over all. In your hand are power and might, and in your hand it is to make great and to give strength to all. 13 And now we thank you, our God, and praise your glorious name.

14 "But who am I, and what is my people, that we should be able thus to offer willingly? For all things come from you, and of your own have we given you. 15 For we are strangers before you and sojourners, as all our fathers were. Our days on the earth are like a shadow, and there is no abiding.[e] 16 O Lord our God, all this abundance that we have provided for building you a house for your holy name comes from your hand and is all your own. 17 I know, my God, that you test the heart and have pleasure in uprightness. In the uprightness of my heart I have freely offered all these things, and now I have seen your people, who are present here, offering freely and joyously to you. 18 O Lord, the God of Abraham, Isaac, and Israel, our fathers, keep forever such purposes and thoughts in the hearts of your people, and direct their hearts toward you. 19 Grant to Solomon my son a whole

LESSON 7:
OUR RESPONSIBILITIES IN THIS AGREEMENT (CON'T)

heart that he may keep your commandments, your testimonies, and your statutes, performing all, and that he may build the palace for which I have made provision."

20 Then David said to all the assembly, "Bless the Lord your God." And all the assembly blessed the Lord, the God of their fathers, and bowed their heads and paid homage to the Lord and to the king. **21** And they offered sacrifices to the Lord, and on the next day offered burnt offerings to the Lord, 1,000 bulls, 1,000 rams, and 1,000 lambs, with their drink offerings, and sacrifices in abundance for all Israel. **22** And they ate and drank before the Lord on that day with great gladness.

Solomon Anointed King
And they made Solomon the son of David king the second time, and they anointed him as prince for the Lord, and Zadok as priest.

23 Then Solomon sat on the throne of the Lord as king in place of David his father. And he prospered, and all Israel obeyed him. **24** All the leaders and the mighty men, and also all the sons of King David, pledged their allegiance to King Solomon. **25** And the Lord made Solomon very great in the sight of all Israel and bestowed on him such royal majesty as had not been on any king before him in Israel.

The Death of David
26 Thus David the son of Jesse reigned over all Israel. **27** The time that he reigned over Israel was forty years. He reigned seven years in Hebron and thirty-three years in Jerusalem. **28** Then he died at a good age, full of days, riches, and honor. And Solomon his son reigned in his place. **29** Now the acts of King David, from first to last, are written in the Chronicles of Samuel the seer, and in the Chronicles of Nathan the prophet, and in the Chronicles of Gad the seer, **30** with accounts of all his rule and his might and of the circumstances that came upon him and upon Israel and upon all the kingdoms of the countries.

3 "Behold, I send my messenger, and he will prepare the way before me. And the Lord whom you seek will suddenly come to his temple; and the messenger of the covenant in whom you delight, behold, he is coming, says the Lord of hosts. **2** But who can endure the day of his coming, and who can stand when he appears? For he is like a refiner's fire and like fullers' soap. **3** He will sit as a refiner and purifier of silver, and he will purify the sons of Levi and refine them like gold and silver, and they will bring offerings in righteousness to the Lord.[a] **4** Then the

LESSON 7:
OUR RESPONSIBILITIES IN THIS AGREEMENT (CON'T)

offering of Judah and Jerusalem will be pleasing to the Lord as in the days of old and as in former years.

5 "Then I will draw near to you for judgment. I will be a swift witness against the sorcerers, against the adulterers, against those who swear falsely, against those who oppress the hired worker in his wages, the widow and the fatherless, against those who thrust aside the sojourner, and do not fear me, says the Lord of hosts.

Robbing God

6 "For I the Lord do not change; therefore you, O children of Jacob, are not consumed. 7 From the days of your fathers you have turned aside from my statutes and have not kept them. Return to me, and I will return to you, says the Lord of hosts. But you say, 'How shall we return?' 8 Will man rob God? Yet you are robbing me. But you say, 'How have we robbed you?' In your tithes and contributions. 9 You are cursed with a curse, for you are robbing me, the whole nation of you. 10 Bring the full tithe into the storehouse, that there may be food in my house. And thereby put me to the test, says the Lord of hosts, if I will not open the windows of heaven for you and pour down for you a blessing until there is no more need. 11 I will rebuke the devourer[b] for you, so that it will not destroy the fruits of your soil, and your vine in the field shall not fail to bear, says the Lord of hosts. 12 Then all nations will call you blessed, for you will be a land of delight, says the Lord of hosts. 13 "Your words have been hard against me, says the Lord. But you say, 'How have we spoken against you?' 14 You have said, 'It is vain to serve God. What is the profit of our keeping his charge or of walking as in mourning before the Lord of hosts? 15 And now we call the arrogant blessed. Evildoers not only prosper but they put God to the test and they escape.'"

The Book of Remembrance

16 Then those who feared the Lord spoke with one another. The Lord paid attention and heard them, and a book of remembrance was written before him of those who feared the Lord and esteemed his name. 17 "They shall be mine, says the Lord of hosts, in the day when I make up my treasured possession, and I will spare them as a man spares his son who serves him. 18 Then once more you shall see the distinction between the righteous and the wicked, between one who serves God and one who does not serve him.

LESSON 7:
OUR RESPONSIBILITIES IN THIS AGREEMENT (CON'T)

Read through 2 Corinthians 9:6-15 and write out why it is so important to tithe and with what kind of heart are we to give financially. How does this serve God's purposes and what does it illustrate about our heart? Why is the principle of sowing and reaping in our life of the covenant so important?

The Cheerful Giver

6 The point is this: whoever sows sparingly will also reap sparingly, and whoever sows bountifully[a] will also reap bountifully. 7 Each one must give as he has decided in his heart, not reluctantly or under compulsion, for God loves a cheerful giver. 8 And God is able to make all grace abound to you, so that having all sufficiency[b] in all things at all times, you may abound in every good work. 9 As it is written,

"He has distributed freely, he has given to the poor;
 his righteousness endures forever."

10 He who supplies seed to the sower and bread for food will supply and multiply your seed for sowing and increase the harvest of your righteousness. 11 You will be enriched in every way to be generous in every way, which through us will produce thanksgiving to God. 12 For the ministry of this service is not only supplying the needs of the saints but is also overflowing in many thanksgivings to God. 13 By their approval of this service, they[c] will glorify God because of your submission that comes from your confession of the gospel of Christ, and the generosity of your contribution for them and for all others, 14 while they long for you and pray for you, because of the surpassing grace of God upon you. 15 Thanks be to God for his inexpressible gift!

_____
_____
_____
_____
_____

Word Meanings:

Sow: scatter, seed
Sparingly: abstain
Reap: harvest
Cheerful: joyous, prompt to do anything
Grace: that which affords joy, pleasure, delight, sweetness, charm, loveliness: grace of speech, good will, loving-kindness, favor

LESSON 7:
OUR RESPONSIBILITIES IN THIS AGREEMENT (CON'T)

Make Abound: to exceed a fixed number of measure, to be left over and above a certain number or measure, to be over, to remain, to exist or be at hand in abundance, to be great (abundant), a thing which comes in abundance, or overflows unto one, something falls to the lot of one in large measure

> **Re-read 1 Chronicles 29:10-20 and write out the kind of hearts that God seeks from His children regarding trusting Him as we consider giving. Why will He test us in this? As you consider your heart, how would you evaluate the state of your heart toward generosity and giving? Why?**
>
> David Prays in the Assembly
> [10] Therefore David blessed the Lord in the presence of all the assembly. And David said: "Blessed are you, O Lord, the God of Israel our father, forever and ever. [11] Yours, O Lord, is the greatness and the power and the glory and the victory and the majesty, for all that is in the heavens and in the earth is yours. Yours is the kingdom, O Lord, and you are exalted as head above all. [12] Both riches and honor come from you, and you rule over all. In your hand are power and might, and in your hand it is to make great and to give strength to all. [13] And now we thank you, our God, and praise your glorious name.
>
> [14] "But who am I, and what is my people, that we should be able thus to offer willingly? For all things come from you, and of your own have we given you. [15] For we are strangers before you and sojourners, as all our fathers were. Our days on the earth are like a shadow, and there is no abiding.[a] [16] O Lord our God, all this abundance that we have provided for building you a house for your holy name comes from your hand and is all your own. [17] I know, my God, that you test the heart and have pleasure in uprightness. In the uprightness of my heart I have freely offered all these things, and now I have seen your people, who are present here, offering freely and joyously to you. [18] O Lord, the God of Abraham, Isaac, and Israel, our fathers, keep forever such purposes and thoughts in the hearts of your people, and direct their hearts toward you. [19] Grant to Solomon my son a whole heart that he may keep your commandments, your testimonies, and your statutes, performing all, and that he may build the palace for which I have made provision."
>
> [20] Then David said to all the assembly, "Bless the Lord your God." And all the assembly blessed the Lord, the God of their fathers, and bowed their heads and paid homage to the Lord and to the king.

LESSON 7:
OUR RESPONSIBILITIES IN THIS AGREEMENT (CON'T)

_____
_____
_____
_____
_____

    This principle of generosity is a universal principle of sowing: God is testing our heart regarding whether we truly trust Him as our provider and giver of the covenant life of abundance. Do we sow and offer a tithe of what He gives us (all is from Him) to His work first? And do we do this willingly because we trust, understanding that all is from Him and that He will provide the covenant life, even while testing our heart?

Word Meanings: **Willingly Offered:** to volunteer, to offer free-will offerings
Joy: mirth, gladness, gaiety, pleasure, joy (*of God*), glad result, happy issue

> **Re-read Malachi 3:10-12 and write out those promises God makes to us as we tithe (there are more than one). Though we are told throughout Scripture to never test God in anything, what are we allowed to do regarding this promise? Why? What will he do?**
>
> [10] Bring the full tithe into the storehouse, that there may be food in my house. And thereby put me to the test, says the Lord of hosts, if I will not open the windows of heaven for you and pour down for you a blessing until there is no more need. [11] I will rebuke the devourer[a] for you, so that it will not destroy the fruits of your soil, and your vine in the field shall not fail to bear, says the Lord of hosts. [12] Then all nations will call you blessed, for you will be a land of delight, says the Lord of hosts.

_____
_____
_____
_____
_____

LESSON 7:
OUR RESPONSIBILITIES IN THIS AGREEMENT (CON'T)

Then, here in Malachi 3, He offers us to test Him right back. Everywhere else in Scripture, we are required never to test Him because it puts Him in the position of being God, and it thus limits Him. (He will not let us be God, and He will not act when we demand that He do what we want.) Here He says it is okay to test Him right back as He tests our hearts. If we tithe, He will prove that He will bless us and command the storehouses to be full. Note in verse 12 that He also promises that He will not allow the enemy to steal it. It will remain. All because we sow generously with a willing heart and prove His promise!

Word Meanings:

Test: to examine, try, prove, scrutinize
Be Opened: be let loose, be thrown open
Storehouse: treasure, (*gold, silver, etc.*) store, supplies of food or drink, treasure-house
Destroy: to destroy, corrupt, go to ruin, decay, to be marred, be spoiled, be corrupted, be corrupt, be injured, be ruined, be rotted

---

Read through Galatians 6:7-10 and write out the outcomes of sowing the flesh versus sowing to the Spirit. What is the difference between the two? How would we sow the Spirit daily so that we reap its benefits?

[7] Do not be deceived: God is not mocked, for whatever one sows, that will he also reap. [8] For the one who sows to his own flesh will from the flesh reap corruption, but the one who sows to the Spirit will from the Spirit reap eternal life. [9] And let us not grow weary of doing good, for in due season we will reap, if we do not give up. [10] So then, as we have opportunity, let us do good to everyone, and especially to those who are of the household of faith.

_____
_____
_____
_____
_____

LESSON 7:
OUR RESPONSIBILITIES IN THIS AGREEMENT (CON'T)

We are further not to sow to the flesh but to our spiritual lives, meaning we are not to live by what we decide on our own (self, flesh) but to surrender to the Father and to the Spirit and let Him lead us. (Re-read Romans 8:5-8 which teaches what happens when we put our mind on the flesh: death of the spirit, enmity against God, and cannot please God versus putting mind on the Spirit, which brings life!) Sow things of the Spirit, which means we are to do what the Father has to say, what is His will. Ask yourself, "Am I sensitive to His leading, am I letting peace umpire my life?"

Word Meanings:

Flesh: the sensuous nature of man, "the animal nature"

Decay: corruption, destruction, perishing that which is subject to corruption, what is perishable

Spirit: the third person of the triune God, the Holy Spirit, coequal, coeternal with the Father and the Son, sometimes referred to in a way which emphasizes His personality and character (the Holy Spirit)

Well Being: beautiful, handsome, excellent, eminent, choice, surpassing, precious, useful, suitable, commendable, admirable, beautiful to look at, shapely, magnificent, good, excellent in its nature and characteristics, and therefore well adapted to its ends, genuine, approved, joined to names of men designated by their office, competent, able, such as one ought to be

---

Read through James 3:13-18 and write out why it is so important to sow (as we have learned above) a life of peace? If we do, what kind of wisdom will we receive, and how will we know the difference? Why is this so important to how we live the covenant life?

Wisdom from Above
[13] Who is wise and understanding among you? By his good conduct let him show his works in the meekness of wisdom. [14] But if you have bitter jealousy and selfish ambition in your hearts, do not boast and be false to the truth. [15] This is not the wisdom that comes down from above, but is earthly, unspiritual, demonic. [16] For where jealousy and selfish ambition exist, there will be disorder and every vile practice. [17] But the wisdom from above is first pure, then peaceable, gentle, open to reason, full of mercy and good fruits, impartial and sincere. [18] And a harvest of righteousness is sown in peace by those who make peace.

LESSON 7:
OUR RESPONSIBILITIES IN THIS AGREEMENT (CON'T)

_____
_____
_____
_____
_____

As we sow peace by staying in peace and offering peace, we will know and receive the wisdom from God and not from the world. We will grow to understand that when we are in confusion or headed toward things that irritate, frustrate, annoy, bring hardship, etc. that these things are not of God. God's wisdom is pure, clear, make things come together, are understandable, and trustworthy. We can walk with God step by step. The reaping is a fruit of our sowing.

Word Meanings:

Humility: mildness of disposition, gentleness of spirit, meekness

Wisdom: broad and full of intelligence; used of the knowledge of very diverse matters, the wisdom which belongs to men, specifically the varied knowledge of things human and divine, acquired by acuteness and experience, and summed up in maxims and proverbs, the science and learning, the act of interpreting dreams and always giving the sagest advice, the intelligence evinced in discovering the meaning of some mysterious number or vision, skill in the management of affairs, devout and proper prudence in intercourse with men not disciples of Christ, skill and discretion in imparting Christian truth, the knowledge and practice of the requisites for godly and upright living

From Above: from a higher place, of things which come from heaven or God, from the first, from the beginning, anew, over again

Sown in Peace: shalom

By Those Making Peace: to make, with the names of things made, to produce, construct, form, fashion, etc., to be the authors of, the cause

Build Fortified Cities:

Read through 2 Chronicles 14:2-8 and write out what Asa did after God had given him rest from battles. What was the purpose of this? How can you apply this in your life?

² And Asa did what was good and right in the eyes of the Lord his God. ³ He took away the foreign altars and the high places and broke down the pillars and cut down the Asherim ⁴ and commanded Judah to seek the Lord, the God of their

LESSON 7:
OUR RESPONSIBILITIES IN THIS AGREEMENT (CON'T)

> fathers, and to keep the law and the commandment. ⁵ He also took out of all the cities of Judah the high places and the incense altars. And the kingdom had rest under him. ⁶ He built fortified cities in Judah, for the land had rest. He had no war in those years, for the Lord gave him peace. ⁷ And he said to Judah, "Let us build these cities and surround them with walls and towers, gates and bars. The land is still ours, because we have sought the Lord our God. We have sought him, and he has given us peace on every side." So they built and prospered. ⁸ And Asa had an army of 300,000 from Judah, armed with large shields and spears, and 280,000 men from Benjamin that carried shields and drew bows. All these were mighty men of valor.

_____
_____
_____
_____

  As Asa did what was good and right in the sight of the Lord, he was called to build fortified cities with walls, towers, bars, gates. But when did they build? After God had given them rest. So, they built as they had a period of rest and no major battles; and did not get lazy and passive but while they had rest took the time and energy to fortify and to strengthen, and as a result, they prospered. Think through what type of things we are to fortify.

  To do this, we must first ask God. It can be things such as abiding time with Him; relationships (marriage, children, extended family); businesses; finances; ministries and non-profit organizations; health; recreation; margin; taking vacations; exercise and physical condition; physical assets, such as houses, etc., or anything that He is laying on our heart.

Word Meanings:

Build: rebuild, establish, cause to continue
No War: battle: rest, settle down and remain, to repose, have rest, be quiet
Prospered: to advance, make progress, succeed, be profitable, to make prosperous, bring to successful issue, cause to prosper, to show or experience prosperity

LESSON 7:
OUR RESPONSIBILITIES IN THIS AGREEMENT (CON'T)

> **Read through Nehemiah 2:17-20 and write out what Nehemiah did as he was called to rebuild the ruined city. In what ways did he trust God, and why was this so important to the building process? What did he expect through the building process? Why?**
>
> [17] Then I said to them, "You see the trouble we are in, how Jerusalem lies in ruins with its gates burned. Come, let us build the wall of Jerusalem, that we may no longer suffer derision." [18] And I told them of the hand of my God that had been upon me for good, and also of the words that the king had spoken to me. And they said, "Let us rise up and build." So they strengthened their hands for the good work. [19] But when Sanballat the Horonite and Tobiah the Ammonite servant and Geshem the Arab heard of it, they jeered at us and despised us and said, "What is this thing that you are doing? Are you rebelling against the king?" [20] Then I replied to them, "The God of heaven will make us prosper, and we his servants will arise and build, but you have no portion or right or claim[a] in Jerusalem."

_____
_____
_____
_____
_____

Nehemiah was called to build the wall and the city of Jerusalem. They had been destroyed by Nebuchadnezzar about 140 years earlier when he attacked the city after God brought judgment during Jeremiah's time. What did we learn were the keys to building and fortifying?

1. Get to it—rise and build—put our hands to the good work directed by God.

2. Do not fret because of opposition (the enemy will attempt to discourage and thwart God's will).

3. Understand it is God's work, and He will prosper the building/fortifying.

LESSON 7:
OUR RESPONSIBILITIES IN THIS AGREEMENT (CON'T)

Word Meanings:

Rise: arise, stand, rise up, stand up, become powerful

Build: rebuild, establish, cause to continue

Good: constitution or nature, useful, salutary, pleasant, agreeable, joyful, happy, excellent, distinguished, upright, honorable

Prosper: to advance, make progress, succeed, be profitable, to make prosperous, bring to successful issue, cause to prosper, to show or experience prosperity

> **Read through 1 Corinthians 3:9-16 and write out that which we are to build upon. Why? What does this practically mean as we are building out the things of our lives? What are the consequences if we do and if we do not?**
>
> 9 For we are God's fellow workers. You are God's field, God's building. 10 According to the grace of God given to me, like a skilled[a] master builder I laid a foundation, and someone else is building upon it. Let each one take care how he builds upon it. 11 For no one can lay a foundation other than that which is laid, which is Jesus Christ. 12 Now if anyone builds on the foundation with gold, silver, precious stones, wood, hay, straw— 13 each one's work will become manifest, for the Day will disclose it, because it will be revealed by fire, and the fire will test what sort of work each one has done. 14 If the work that anyone has built on the foundation survives, he will receive a reward. 15 If anyone's work is burned up, he will suffer loss, though he himself will be saved, but only as through fire.
> 16 Do you not know that you[b] are God's temple and that God's Spirit dwells in you?

_____
_____
_____
_____
_____

The key will be to build where He so directs. He is the master builder, so we are only to build on His foundation, and on nothing else, otherwise anything we build will be worthless and have no value (both temporal and eternal). The most important key is to build only where and how He tells us to build and not what we think is a good idea. If we do not, there will be eternal consequences. Imagine at the end of our Earthly life that we are before Christ and He either says well done,

LESSON 7:
OUR RESPONSIBILITIES IN THIS AGREEMENT (CON'T)

you built and fortified where I asked you to build (my assignments for you) or He says that what you built was wood and hay stubble, both of which are worthless because you did it on your own. This is critical and most significant. Realize how we will feel to hear what He has to say about our assignments of building and fortifying, as both truly have eternal consequences.

Word Meanings:

Building: building up, metaphorically edifying, edification, the act of one who promotes another's growth in Christian wisdom, piety, happiness, holiness, a building (i.e. the thing built, edifice)

A Master Builder: an architect, the superintendent in the erection of buildings

Foundations: beginnings, first principals, of institution or system of truth

Prove: to test, examine, scrutinize (to see whether a thing is genuine or not), as metals, to recognize as genuine after examination, to approve, deem worthy

Rewards: which God bestows, or will bestow, upon good deeds and endeavors

LESSON 8:
CALLED TO GIVE IT AWAY (BE A BLESSING)

GIVE IT AWAY.

Since the essence of the covenant is to be "blessed to be a blessing," we are called to "give it away."

> **Read through Luke 1:67-80 and write out the very reasons that Christ came to mankind. How are we to join Him in this purpose in our lives?**
>
> Zechariah's Prophecy
> 67 And his father Zechariah was filled with the Holy Spirit and prophesied, saying,
> 68 "Blessed be the Lord God of Israel,
>   for he has visited and redeemed his people
> 69 and has raised up a horn of salvation for us
>   in the house of his servant David,
> 70 as he spoke by the mouth of his holy prophets from of old,
> 71 that we should be saved from our enemies
>   and from the hand of all who hate us;
> 72 to show the mercy promised to our fathers
>   and to remember his holy covenant,
> 73 the oath that he swore to our father Abraham, to grant us
> 74   that we, being delivered from the hand of our enemies, might serve him without fear,
> 75   in holiness and righteousness before him all our days.
> 76 And you, child, will be called the prophet of the Most High;
>   for you will go before the Lord to prepare his ways,
> 77 to give knowledge of salvation to his people
>   in the forgiveness of their sins,
> 78 because of the tender mercy of our God,
>   whereby the sunrise shall visit us[a] from on high
> 79 to give light to those who sit in darkness and in the shadow of death, to guide our feet into the way of peace."
>
> 80 And the child grew and became strong in spirit, and he was in the wilderness until the day of his public appearance to Israel.

> "We are to let Him lead and guide only. We are never to question His assignments and especially the size, what we might consider the importance, etc."

LESSON 8:
CALLED TO GIVE IT AWAY (BE A BLESSING)

_____
_____
_____
_____
_____
_____

The very life of Christ was purposed to remember the covenant: bless us to make us a blessing by:

1. Delivering us from the enemy

2. Serving Him in holiness and righteousness (fruit)

3. Giving salvation (wholeness, completeness – the gospel)

4. Giving light to those in darkness

5. Guiding us onto the steps (the way) of shalom.

Since Christ is in us, we are to join Him in this work of the covenant and understand this grand purpose in giving it away.

Word Meanings: **Give:** to give something to someone, of one's own accord to give one something, to his advantage, to bestow a gift, to grant, give to one asking, let have, to supply, furnish, necessary things, to give over, deliver, to reach out, extend, present
Knowledge: signifies in general intelligence, understanding, the general knowledge of Christian religion, the deeper more perfect and enlarged knowledge of this religion, such as belongs to the more advanced
Shine Upon: to show to or upon, to bring to light, to appear, become visible, of stars, to become clearly known, to show one's self
Darkness: of ignorance respecting divine things and human duties, and the accompanying ungodliness and immorality, together with their consequent misery in hell, persons in whom darkness becomes visible and holds sway

LESSON 8:
CALLED TO GIVE IT AWAY (BE A BLESSING)

> Read through John 20:19-23 and write out what Jesus said to His disciples (and thus to us) as to how we are to carry out His purposes here in this world. How does this exactly work? What precisely does this mean in your life now?
>
> Jesus Appears to the Disciples
> [19] On the evening of that day, the first day of the week, the doors being locked where the disciples were for fear of the Jews,[a] Jesus came and stood among them and said to them, "Peace be with you." [20] When he had said this, he showed them his hands and his side. Then the disciples were glad when they saw the Lord. [21] Jesus said to them again, "Peace be with you. As the Father has sent me, even so I am sending you." [22] And when he had said this, he breathed on them and said to them, "Receive the Holy Spirit. [23] If you forgive the sins of any, they are forgiven them; if you withhold forgiveness from any, it is withheld."

_____
_____
_____
_____
_____

    As Christ was sent, so is He sending us. How was He sent? By doing only what the Father said and showed Him. So, as we give it away, we are not to do anything on our own (what we think are good ideas in giving it away). Rather only when, where, and with whom we are to give it away as directed by the Father. We are to let Him lead and guide only. We are never to question His assignments and especially the size, what we might consider the importance, etc. All are significant and best because we are part of His bigger story, and we cannot understand the impact of the part it plays in the totality of the bigger and broader story, especially the longer term.

Word Meanings: **Peace:** shalom
Sent: to order (one) to go to a place appointed, to send away, that he may be in a state of liberty

LESSON 8:
CALLED TO GIVE IT AWAY (BE A BLESSING)

> **Read through Acts 1:5-8 and write out Jesus' command for all of us regarding our assignment for the Kingdom of God. How is this to be carried out? What does this mean to us practically right now?**
>
> 5 for John baptized with water, but you will be baptized with[a] the Holy Spirit not many days from now."
> The Ascension
> 6 So when they had come together, they asked him, "Lord, will you at this time restore the kingdom to Israel?" 7 He said to them, "It is not for you to know times or seasons that the Father has fixed by his own authority. 8 But you will receive power when the Holy Spirit has come upon you, and you will be my witnesses in Jerusalem and in all Judea and Samaria, and to the end of the earth."

_____
_____
_____
_____
_____

    We are called to be His witnesses. This is a legal term to be called on the stand when He calls us up to testify as to what we have experienced; not hearsay (preaching about Christ), but what we ourselves experience, and why living in the covenant is so important. We have to be blessed in order to be a blessing to others, to be able to give it away. And, we do not have to have a program or a set agenda to be a witness--only as He calls upon us to be a witness and give it away. This is why we can relax and enjoy life with a heart to give it away, and then give it away freely as we are called. This giving will be a joy with no burden.

Word Meanings: **Receive:** to take with the hand, lay hold of, any person or thing in order to use it, to take up a thing to be carried, to take upon one's self, to take in order to carry away, to take what is one's own, to take to one's self, to make one's own
Power: dunamis
Witness: in a legal sense, an historical sense, one who is a spectator of anything, e.g. of a contest

LESSON 8:
CALLED TO GIVE IT AWAY (BE A BLESSING)

> **Read through Acts 2:40-47 and write out how the early church "gave it away" as they gathered together. Why were people attracted to what they were doing and experiencing and thus what happened daily? How might we practice this today with our Christian gatherings?**
>
> ⁴⁰ And with many other words he bore witness and continued to exhort them, saying, "Save yourselves from this crooked generation." ⁴¹ So those who received his word were baptized, and there were added that day about three thousand souls.
>
> The Fellowship of the Believers
> ⁴² And they devoted themselves to the apostles' teaching and the fellowship, to the breaking of bread and the prayers. ⁴³ And awe[a] came upon every soul, and many wonders and signs were being done through the apostles. ⁴⁴ And all who believed were together and had all things in common. ⁴⁵ And they were selling their possessions and belongings and distributing the proceeds to all, as any had need. ⁴⁶ And day by day, attending the temple together and breaking bread in their homes, they received their food with glad and generous hearts, ⁴⁷ praising God and having favor with all the people. And the Lord added to their number day by day those who were being saved.

_____
_____
_____
_____
_____

Walk through this description of the early church, which describes the beauty and joy of giving it away:

1. Be in the Word and fellowship (in the Spirit) regularly
2. Break bread together
3. Pray together (dialoguing and listening to God)
4. Experience signs and wonders (miracles, mighty works of God)
5. Share things and help each other financially
6. Give away with gladness and simplicity of heart

LESSON 8:
CALLED TO GIVE IT AWAY (BE A BLESSING)

As a result, the Lord added people daily! Others experience how they were being blessed (they were in awe at the supernatural) and others wanted to experience it as well. They freely gave away what they were receiving—covenant!

Word Meanings:

Teaching: that which is taught, doctrine, concerning something, the act of teaching, instruction

Fellowship: association, community, communion, joint participation, intercourse, the share which one has in anything, fellowship, intimacy

Wonders: a prodigy, portent, miracle (*performed by any one*)

Sign: mark, token, that by which a person or a thing is distinguished from others and is known, a sign, prodigy, portent, i.e. an unusual occurrence, transcending the common course of nature, of signs portending remarkable events soon to happen, of miracles and wonders by which God authenticates the men sent by Him, or by which men prove that the cause they are pleading is God's

One Accord: with one mind, with one accord, with one passion, unique Greek word, used 10 of its 12 New Testament occurrences in the Book of Acts, helps us understand the uniqueness of the Christian community. Homothumadon is a compound of two words meaning to "rush along" and "in unison." The image is almost musical; a number of notes are sounded which, while different, harmonize in pitch and tone. As the instruments of a great concert are under the direction of a concert master, so the Holy Spirit blends together the lives of members of Christ's church.

> **Read through 2 Timothy 2:1-2 and write out what Paul instructed us to do in sharing what we are learning with others. How do we carry this out? With whom in our lives can we begin to share what we are learning?**
>
> A Good Soldier of Christ Jesus
> **2** You then, my child, be strengthened by the grace that is in Christ Jesus, ² and what you have heard from me in the presence of many witnesses entrust to faithful men,[a] who will be able to teach others also.

_____
_____
_____
_____
_____

LESSON 8:
CALLED TO GIVE IT AWAY (BE A BLESSING)

As we give it away, we are to have discernment, so that as we give it away, we are entrusting that what we are giving away to others will also then be given away. How would we know that? By them demonstrating that they are abiding, experiencing the covenant, and beginning to give it away themselves. It will not take long to see that this is true. If so, continue to give it away. If those you are giving to don't seem to be interested, move on and give away to others. They will be lining up around the block to receive what you have to give away. Remember it is critical that you are living in the covenant to be able to give it away—blessed to be a blessing.

Word Meanings:

Entrust: to place beside or near or set before, food, i.e. food placed on a table, to set before (*one*) in teaching, to set forth (*from one's self*), to explain, to place down (*from one's self or for one's self*) with any one, to deposit, to entrust, commit to one's charge

Faithful: of persons who show themselves faithful in the transaction of business, the execution of commands, or the discharge of official duties, one who kept his plighted faith, worthy of trust that can be relied on

REMEMBER, HE WORKS BOTH SIDES OF THE AGREEMENT!

Now that you have walked through all of the requirements of what is our part of the agreement, we now reinforce that God works both sides of the agreement. It really is not our work on our own, but rather because He lives in us, it is His work. These verses will show us the power of this.

> **Read through Jeremiah 31:31-34 and write out the truths about the role of the Holy Spirit. What does He promise to do as work to carry out our part of the covenant agreement? Why is this such an important truth and so critical to our meeting this condition?**
>
> The New Covenant
> ³¹ "Behold, the days are coming, declares the Lord, when I will make a new covenant with the house of Israel and the house of Judah, ³² not like the covenant that I made with their fathers on the day when I took them by the hand to bring them out of the land of Egypt, my covenant that they broke, though I was their husband, declares the Lord. ³³ For this is the covenant that I will make with the house of Israel after those days, declares the Lord: I will put my law within them, and I will write it on their hearts. And I will be their God, and they shall be my

LESSON 8:
CALLED TO GIVE IT AWAY (BE A BLESSING)

> people. ³⁴ And no longer shall each one teach his neighbor and each his brother, saying, 'Know the Lord,' for they shall all know me, from the least of them to the greatest, declares the Lord. For I will forgive their iniquity, and I will remember their sin no more."

_____

_____

_____

_____

_____

The new covenant is Christ in us through the Holy Spirit, which will:

1. Put the requirements in our minds and hearts
2. Not need to be taught by others but will be taught by the Holy Spirit

He will cause us to have the power to be able to live out the requirements to meet the conditions of the covenant. He will instruct us and then give us the power to be obedient to the instructions.

Word Meanings:

Write: record, enroll, to write, inscribe, engrave, write in, write on, to write down, describe in writing, to register, to decree

Hearts: inner man, mind, will, understanding, inner part, midst, midst (of things), heart (of man), soul, heart (of man) mind, knowledge, thinking, reflection, memory, inclination, resolution, determination (of will)

Inward Parts: midst, among, inner part, middle, physical sense, as seat of thought and emotion, as faculty of thought and emotion

> **Read Jeremiah 32:37-42.**
>
> ³⁷ Behold, I will gather them from all the countries to which I drove them in my anger and my wrath and in great indignation. I will bring them back to this place, and I will make them dwell in safety. ³⁸ And they shall be my people, and I will be their God. ³⁹ I will give them one heart and one way, that they may fear me forever, for their own good and the good of their children after them. ⁴⁰ I will

LESSON 8:
CALLED TO GIVE IT AWAY (BE A BLESSING)

> make with them an everlasting covenant, that I will not turn away from doing good to them. And I will put the fear of me in their hearts, that they may not turn from me. [41] I will rejoice in doing them good, and I will plant them in this land in faithfulness, with all my heart and all my soul.
>
> [42] "For thus says the Lord: Just as I have brought all this great disaster upon this people, so I will bring upon them all the good that I promise them.

_____
_____
_____
_____
_____

These things we will be given while the Spirit is with us:

1. One heart (His heart)
2. One way (His way)
3. A fear of Him (trust and believe Him, that the promises are true and real; and that His instructions are best and none better; and that we will be given the power to be obedient to the instructions)
4. The delivery of the covenant—everlasting good
5. A constant walk with Him so that we stay in the Kingdom and thus receive the covenant
6. The knowledge that He will rejoice over doing us good by delivering the covenant.

Word Meanings: **Put Good:** to be good, be pleasing, be joyful, be beneficial, be pleasant, be favorable, be happy, be right, be delightful, to be glad, to be better, to be well with, be good for, to do well, do good, act right, act rightly
Bring: to come to pass

LESSON 8:
CALLED TO GIVE IT AWAY (BE A BLESSING)

AND: WE RECEIVE THE DESIRES OF OUR HEART!

As we walk with Him in the Kingdom and enjoy the benefits of the covenant, He will give us the desires of our hearts. The circumstances of our life will line up to thrill our hearts as He so made us and that are unique to us. Remember, these are not to be chased because He will give these to us. He has a lifetime to give these, and since they are from Him, He will refine the depth and profound understanding of what they truly are so our desires are truly met. It will be a lifetime of surprises and giving us circumstances and things that thrill us and excite us—all part of the covenant blessings.

> **Read through Psalm 37:3-8 and write out what is promised if we delight ourselves in God (meet the conditions of the covenant). What are these conditions as stated here? Where do you need to adjust to meet these conditions to delight yourself in God?**
>
> ³ Trust in the Lord, and do good;
>   dwell in the land and befriend faithfulness.[a]
> ⁴ Delight yourself in the Lord,
>   and he will give you the desires of your heart.
> ⁵ Commit your way to the Lord;
>   trust in him, and he will act.
> ⁶ He will bring forth your righteousness as the light,
>   and your justice as the noonday.
> ⁷ Be still before the Lord and wait patiently for him;
>   fret not yourself over the one who prospers in his way,
>   over the man who carries out evil devices!
> ⁸ Refrain from anger, and forsake wrath!
>   Fret not yourself; it tends only to evil.

_____
_____
_____
_____
_____

LESSON 8:
CALLED TO GIVE IT AWAY (BE A BLESSING)

He will give us the desires of our hearts as we meet the condition of delighting in Him through meeting the key conditions.

Conditions: trust Him; dwell in Him (abide); delight in Him.

Word Meanings:

Trust: have confidence, to be bold
Good: constitution or nature, useful, salutary, pleasant, agreeable, joyful, happy, excellent, distinguished, upright, honorable
Dwell: abide, reside
Feed: pasture, tend, graze
Delight: to be happy about, take exquisite delight, to make merry over
Heart: inner man, mind, will, soul, understanding
Commit: roll down same path
Come to Pass: make happen
Rest: to be silent, be still
Wait: dance with

Read Psalm 21:1-7.

The King Rejoices in the Lord's Strength
To the choirmaster. A Psalm of David.
21 O Lord, in your strength the king rejoices,
   and in your salvation how greatly he exults!
² You have given him his heart's desire
   and have not withheld the request of his lips. Selah
³ For you meet him with rich blessings;
   you set a crown of fine gold upon his head.
⁴ He asked life of you; you gave it to him,
   length of days forever and ever.
⁵ His glory is great through your salvation;
   splendor and majesty you bestow on him.
⁶ For you make him most blessed forever;[a]
   you make him glad with the joy of your presence.
⁷ For the king trusts in the Lord,
   and through the steadfast love of the Most High he shall not be moved.

LESSON 8:
CALLED TO GIVE IT AWAY (BE A BLESSING)

_____
_____
_____
_____
_____

Conditions: we asked Him; we trust Him and then are met with blessings and goodness, honor and majesty (exciting life).

Word Meanings: **Give:** bestow, grant, permit, ascribe, employ, devote, consecrate, dedicate, pay wages, sell, exchange, lend, commit, entrust, give over, deliver up, yield produce, occasion, produce, requite to, report, mention, utter, stretch out, extend, to put, set, put on, put upon, appoint, assign, designate
Desires: wish, longings of one's heart, lust, appetite, covetousness (bad sense), thing desired, object of desire
Goodness: good constitution or nature, useful, salutary, pleasant, agreeable, joyful, happy, excellent, distinguished, upright, honorable
Majesty: ornament, splendor, honor, glory
Gladness: joy, mirth, gladness, gaiety, pleasure, joy (of God), glad result, happy issue

---

Read Psalm 20:1-6.

Trust in the Name of the Lord Our God
To the choirmaster. A Psalm of David.
20 May the Lord answer you in the day of trouble!
  May the name of the God of Jacob protect you!
² May he send you help from the sanctuary
  and give you support from Zion!
³ May he remember all your offerings
  and regard with favor your burnt sacrifices! Selah
⁴ May he grant you your heart's desire
  and fulfill all your plans!

LESSON 8:
CALLED TO GIVE IT AWAY (BE A BLESSING)

> ⁵ May we shout for joy over your salvation,
>   and in the name of our God set up our banners!
>   May the Lord fulfill all your petitions!
> ⁶ Now I know that the Lord saves his anointed;
>   he will answer him from his holy heaven
>   with the saving might of his right hand.

_____
_____
_____
_____
_____

Conditions: offerings and burnt sacrifice (repentance); set up banner in the name of the Lord (stood on our witness and faith in God without compromise); petitions (talked to God in prayer).

Word Meanings: **Fulfill:** to fill, be full, to be full, fullness, abundance (participle), be accomplished, be ended
Desires: request, petition

Read through Psalm 145 (OUR MISSION) and write out all the details required of our mission of living out the covenant of God. How are we to adjust our lives to carry out this mission?

Great Is the Lord
ᵃA Song of Praise. Of David.
145 I will extol you, my God and King,
  and bless your name forever and ever.
² Every day I will bless you
  and praise your name forever and ever.
³ Great is the Lord, and greatly to be praised,
  and his greatness is unsearchable.
⁴ One generation shall commend your works to another,
  and shall declare your mighty acts.

LESSON 8:
CALLED TO GIVE IT AWAY (BE A BLESSING)

⁵ On the glorious splendor of your majesty,
    and on your wondrous works, I will meditate.
⁶ They shall speak of the might of your awesome deeds,
    and I will declare your greatness.
⁷ They shall pour forth the fame of your abundant goodness
    and shall sing aloud of your righteousness.
⁸ The Lord is gracious and merciful,
    slow to anger and abounding in steadfast love.
⁹ The Lord is good to all,
    and his mercy is over all that he has made.
¹⁰ All your works shall give thanks to you, O Lord,
    and all your saints shall bless you!
¹¹ They shall speak of the glory of your kingdom
    and tell of your power,
¹² to make known to the children of man your[b] mighty deeds,
    and the glorious splendor of your kingdom.
¹³ Your kingdom is an everlasting kingdom,
    and your dominion endures throughout all generations.
[The Lord is faithful in all his words
    and kind in all his works.][c]
¹⁴ The Lord upholds all who are falling
    and raises up all who are bowed down.
¹⁵ The eyes of all look to you,
    and you give them their food in due season.
¹⁶ You open your hand;
    you satisfy the desire of every living thing.
¹⁷ The Lord is righteous in all his ways
    and kind in all his works.
¹⁸ The Lord is near to all who call on him,
    to all who call on him in truth.
¹⁹ He fulfills the desire of those who fear him;
    he also hears their cry and saves them.
²⁰ The Lord preserves all who love him,
    but all the wicked he will destroy.
²¹ My mouth will speak the praise of the Lord,
    and let all flesh bless his holy name forever and ever.

LESSON 8:
CALLED TO GIVE IT AWAY (BE A BLESSING)

_____
_____
_____
_____
_____

Psalm 145 gives us our mission now that we understand we are called to the covenant—blessed to be a blessing:

1. Bless the Name of the Lord always
2. Praise the wonderful works and declare His mighty miracles, awesome acts, and the memory of His great goodness to the next generation (tell of His wonderful covenant blessings)
3. Speak of the glory of His Kingdom, as His dominion endures forever
4. Keep looking to Him in hope with expectation; knowing He satisfies our desires—as we call upon Him in truth. Stay surrendered and keep seeking the truth of His will
5. Praise and bless His Holy Name

Be blessed, bless others and bring the glory to God. What a wonderful place to live—the covenant!

Word Meanings: **Be Marvelous:** be wonderful, be surpassing, be extraordinary, separate by distinguishing action, to be beyond one's power, be difficult to do, to be difficult to understand
Desire: pleasure, delight, favor, goodwill, acceptance, will, desire, self-will

www.ingramcontent.com/pod-product-compliance
Lightning Source LLC
Chambersburg PA
CBHW051256110526
44589CB00025B/2854